JN426561

English Up Book 2

Kyungbok University Language Education Center

Series Editors: *Bo Taig Kwon, Curtis MacDonald*

Series Authors: *Alun Cave, Kristina Chang, Anthony Kaschor, Bo Taig Kwon, Bridget Leathwick, Curtis MacDonald, Jamese Newkirk, Julien Poncet, Kenneth Robertson, William Sharp, Jordan Stewart, Hugo Titman, Don Urban*

도서출판 동인

Published by Dongin Publishing Co.
#118, 3-5 Hyehwa-ro, Jongno-gu, Seoul, Korea (03075)
Tel: (02) 765-7145, Fax: (02) 765-7165, Email: dongin60@chollian.net, Homepage: donginbook.co.kr

ISBN 978-89-5506-709-5　　13740

정가 : 20,000 원

Table of Contents

WELCOME TO ENGLISH UP BOOK 2

MEET THE AUTHORS:

Alun Cave

Alun Cave has been an EFL teacher in Korea since 2003. In addition to providing language education to thousands of students, he also promotes continuous professional development, and has organized workshops on the use of technology in the classroom. As one of the founding members of the English program at Kyungbok University, Alun Cave has helped bring KBU's Language Education Center to the forefront of English instruction in Korea. He also has a great sense of humour.

Kristina Chang

Kristina Chang is currently a professor at Kyungbok University. Before coming to Korea, she worked as a research scientist in the University of Washington School of Medicine for four years. Subsequently, she has a background in scientific writing and has published twice in the Journal of Virology. She is fluent in both English and Korean and contributes her bilingual background to her ability to understand and teach the fundamental patterns found in language.

Anthony Kaschor

Anthony Kaschor is currently lecturing at Kyungbok University in South Korea. Since 2003, he has written material for various publishers of ESL/EFL course books, and taught English learners of all ages and walks of life. As a former graphic designer, he brings his creative side to his classroom. Anthony holds a B. Mgt degree and a MA. TESOL/TEFL degree. He continues to pursue new ways to engage and motivate his students.

Bo Taig Kwon

Bo Taig Kwon taught English and English Literature in Sogang University for 5 years and has been in Kyungbok University since 2001. Based upon his experiences in Newcastle University, England and in Sogang University, he tries to focus on communicative language teaching, let alone basic matters such as vocabulary and intermediate level of grammar.

Bridget Leathwick

Bridget Leathwick has been teaching English in South Korea for the past 8 years. She has taught a wide variety of ages and levels during her time in Korea. This has given her a solid knowledge foundation for her contribution to the book development at Kyungbok University. In her native New Zealand, Bridget is a Registered Nurse. She loves working with people in a supportive and educational role, which both nursing and teaching require.

Curtis MacDonald

Curtis MacDonald has been an English instructor for over a decade, all within Korea. His experiences in and out of the classroom inspire his section of the book. He believes any student can be successful in English. It is his hope that students can restart their studies in a fun and meaningful way in this book.

Jamese Newkirk

Jamese Newkirk has been teaching English as a second language to students from various cultural backgrounds and academic abilities for 8 years. She has lived and taught in South Korea for 6 years and contributed to several curriculum development projects. Jamese has her BA in Political Science and a Masters in Education. She is also a lifetime learner and continues to educate herself in a multitude of academic fields.

Julien Poncet

Julien Poncet started teaching English as a second language in Boston, USA, almost 10 years ago. His students came from all around the world, especially South Korea. It is based on their recommendation that he decided to pursue his teaching adventure in Korea, which he now calls home.

Kenneth Robertson

Kenneth Robertson hails from Scotland, UK. During his 9 years in Korea, he has taught ESL to various levels and ages of students. The majority of his experience has been with elementary students. He looks forward to living and working in Korea for many years to come.

William Sharp

William Sharp has a strong background in language teaching and takes great pride in his ability to develop a strong rapport with his students. He holds a B.A. in Arts (Literature and Mandarin) from Western University in Sydney, Australia. He also holds a B.A. in Teaching and is fully certified by the NSW Board of Studies and Department of Education and Communities. As a career teacher and lifelong learner, William understands the importance of a positive learning environment and always maintains high expectations of his students.

Jordan Stewart

Jordan Stewart began teaching English for the Daejeon (South Korea) Metropolitan Office of Education in 2008. He has taught elementary and middle school students, and public school faculty, and currently teaches at Kyungbok University. Jordan holds a BS degree in Computer Science from the University of Hawaii.

Hugo Titman

Hugo Titman's educational background is in the Classics, Librarianship and Business Studies. He has used his 10 years of experience as an ESL teacher collaborating with Chinese and South Korean students of all ages, backgrounds and levels to help them grasp English grammar and usage and to provide them with good opportunities to hear, read, speak and write English. He enjoys building and maintaining strong communicative bridges between himself and his class, and between students in his class.

Don Urban

Don Urban hails from Cobalt, Ontario and is a graduate of Bishop's University. He has taught at every level in the Korean education system. His passion for technology and internet learning has enhanced the lives of countless students. Professor Urban has a strong background in history and sociology and uses those skills to bring a deep cultural awareness to any lecture or class. A strong believer that a teacher is always a student, he constantly challenges himself to learn and improve his teaching methods.

WELCOME UNIT:

Welcome to the English Up Series. This series was created to give everyone, from false beginner to high intermediate, a chance to be successful in English. It has several interesting features.

A. **Warm-up Questions:** This section is to prepare the student for talking using common questions and helping the student to speak in full sentences. The secondary goal is to prepare the students for a job interview, whether it be in response to common questions or in self introduction form.
기본 질문: 이 부분은 학생들로 하여금 일상적인 질문을 활용하여 대화할 수 있도록 준비시키고 온전한 문장으로 말할 수 있게 도와주는 부분입니다. 두 번째 목적은 입사면접에서 활용할 수 있는 일상적 질문에 관한 답변 또는 자기소개를 할 수 있게 준비시키는 것입니다.

B. **Dialogues:** The dialogue section is to give the student exposure to real conversation and, combined with the substitution exercise, to allow the student to prepare and practice the conversations. The substitution exercise will allow for flexibility in conversation and an increase in vocabulary. In many cases, the replaced dialogue piece is a common slang or colloquial, which are often hard to understand to the second language learner.
대화: 대화 부분은 학생들로 하여금 실생활에 활용되는 회화를 접할 수 있게 해 주고 대입식의 방법을 활용하여 학생들이 회화를 준비하고 연습할 수 있도록 해 줍니다. 대입연습을 통해 대화시 융통성을 발휘할 수 있고 어휘력을 증진시킬 수 있습니다. 대체하여 사용하는 회화표현은 일상적인 속어 또는 구어체 표현인데 외국어로 영어를 배우는 학생들이 이해하기에 종종 어려운 경우가 많습니다.

C. **Conversation Corner:** This section helps to prepare the student for a real world conversation, both in the workplace and on the street. The secondary goal is to teach the students how to be respectful and use honorifics in English.
대화 부분: 이 부분은 직장이나 거리에서 발생할 수 있는 실제 상황에 대처할 수 있는 능력을 향상시킵니다. 두 번째 목적은 영어에서 경칭과 존대말을 사용하는 방법을 가르치는 것입니다.

D. **Grammar Gallery:** The grammar starts at the basic level and builds up to cover most of the major tenses in English. Beyond using a pattern and repeating it, the grammar gallary compares and contrasts grammar in regard to usage and helps the student to recognize not only how to use the grammar, but when to use the grammar. This section will also reflect the grammar questions used in the TOEIC test whenever possible.
문법 부분: 기본 사항을 위시하여 영어의 대부분의 시제를 다루게 됩니다. 문형 반복 훈련을 뛰어넘어 용법과 관련한 비교와 대조를 하면서 학생들이 문법을 언제 어떻게 활용해야 하는지를 느끼게 지도합니다. 이 부분은 또한 가능할 때마다 토익에서 활용되는 문법 문제를 반영합니다.

E. **TOEIC Vocabulary:** One of the biggest factors in mastering a language and a test is the building of vocabulary. This book expects the students to take responsibilty for their own education. We will introduce almost 1,000 new words in this series, words that are frequently used in conversation and in TOEIC. Often these words will be assigned as homework, or self study. It is the student responsibilty to make themselves proficient in the provided vocabulary.
토익 빈출어휘: 외국어 학습과 외국어 시험에서 가장 큰 요소 중 하나는 어휘력 향상입니다. 본 교재는 학생들이 자신의 학습을 스스로 하기를 기대합니다. 회화에 자주 사용되며 토익에도 출제되는 대략 1,000개의 어휘를 이 부분에서 취급합니

다. 이 어휘들은 과제용 또는 자습용입니다. 주어진 어휘를 활용하는 것은 학생들의 몫입니다.

F. **Other:** As the level progresses, different sections such as TOEIC preparation/phrasal verbs and idioms/and career concentration will be added. These will help the student in the growing pyramid of knowledge and help them to understand and use English better.
기타: 단계를 밟아갈수록 토익 준비와 동사구, 숙어 그리고 직업 관련 내용과 같은 새로운 내용이 추가됩니다. 이런 내용은 점점 쌓여만 가는 거대한 지식의 피라미드 속에서 학생들에게 도움을 줄 것이고 영어를 보다 더 잘 이해하고 활용하는 데 도움을 줄 것입니다.

CLASSROOM ETIQUETTE

1. Students are expected to be at their desk with all the appropriate materials (book, pencil, pen, notebook, etc.) at the beginning of class. Being late is disrespectful to the professor and to the students who are ready for class to begin on time.
수업이 시작되면 학생들은 필요한 준비물(교재, 필기구 공책 등)을 지참하고 책상에 앉아있어야 합니다. 지각은 정시에 수업을 시작할 준비가 되어있는 학생 및 교수님에게 실례를 범하는 것입니다.

2. Cell phones can be used in class to help the student understand. There are dictionary translations and certain apps that can expand the student's breadth of knowledge. However, too many students use their phone to text message or surf the internet. Cell phones should be put away out of sight in a bag, not in the desk where it can be easily seen. All learning requires concentration and focus. Recent studies show that looking at the cell phone can disrupt the brain's attention and ability to learn for up to 17 minutes. So please understand that we ask you to put your cell phones away not as a punishment, but as a path to greater learning.
휴대전화는 학생들의 이해를 돕기 위해 활용될 수 있습니다. 학생들의 지식의 폭을 넓힐 수 있는 번역문과 앱이 있습니다. 그러나 너무 많은 학생들이 문자를 보내거나 인터넷 검색을 하기 위해 휴대전화를 사용합니다. 휴대전화는 책상 위에 두지 말고 가방에 보이지 않게 간직해야 합니다. 모든 학습에는 집중이 필요합니다. 최근의 연구에 의하면 휴대전화를 볼 경우 17분 동안 주의를 산만하게 한다고 합니다. 따라서 벌칙이 아니라 더 나은 학습을 위해 휴대전화를 보이지 않는 곳에 간직하라는 지시를 이해해 주기 바랍니다.

3. **Being an effective student:** The instructors can only do so much with the time they are given.
It is the student's responsibility to be prepared to learn and practice the exercises. Each class, the instructor will give you opportunity to answer questions and practice dialogue with partners. Doing these exercises is crucial for improvement, as well as doing any homework assigned.
효과적인 학습을 하기 위해: 교수님들은 강의시간에 최선을 다합니다. 학생들은 배우고 연습할 준비가 되어있어야 합니다. 매 시간 교수님들은 학생들에게 대답할 기회를 줄 것이고 다른 학생들과 대화를 연습하도록 할 것입니다. 이런 연습은 주어진 과제를 수행하는 것만큼 영어실력 향상을 위해 중요한 것입니다.

4. **Have fun:** English does not have to be that daunting subject that causes stress and fear.
It is a language and should be spoken and used to communicate. Be free to laugh and have fun if you make mistakes, as everyone will make mistakes, even native speakers. Enjoying a class can only reinforce the materials that we are trying to give you.
수업을 즐기세요: 영어는 스트레스와 공포를 자아내는 무서운 과목일 필요가 없습니다. 언어일 뿐이고 소통을 하기 위해 말하고 사용하는 것입니다. 누구나 실수하고 심지어 원어민들도 실수를 하니까 실수를 하더라도 자유롭게 웃고 즐기세요. 수업을 즐기면 교수님들이 학생들에게 제공하는 내용을 더 잘 이해할 수 있을 것입니다.

MEET THE CHARACTERS:

P. K. Olivier

- Gender: Male
- Birthday: October 30, 1982
- Age: 34
- Phone number: Home: 031-7656-8215
  Cell: 010-8622-5494
- Address: 75 Sunhwagung-ro Street, Namyangju, Gyeonggi-do,
  South Korea, 12019
- Country of Birth: South Africa
- Family: Wife (Rebecca Olivier / Birthday: June 7, 1987 / 29 years old)
  1 son (Karl Olivier / Birthday: July 13th, 2009 / 7 years old)

Michelle Lacroix

- Gender: Female
- Birthday: July 22, 1996
- Age: 20
- Phone number: Home: 031-4549-2185
  Cell: 010-8666-8209
- Address: 6 Buma-ro Street, Namyangju, Gyeonggi-do,
  South Korea, 12019
- Country of Birth: Canada
- Family: Orphan

Tiffiny O'Neal

- Gender: Female
- Birthday: February 2, 1990
- Age: 26
- Phone number: Home 031-505-5000
  Cell: 010-4108-2008
- Address: 192 Simin-ro Street, Uijeongbu, Gyeonggi-do,
  South Korea, 11728
- Country of Birth: U.S.A.
- Family: Husband (John O'Neal / Birthday: May 10, 1985 /
  31 years old / works at a smartphone company)
  1 dog (Munch / Birthday: June 1, 2010 / 6 years old /
  French bulldog)

Marco Agudelo

- Gender: Male
- Birthday: July 23, 1981
- Age: 35
- Phone number: Home 02-3598-9080
  Cell: 010-3584-9834
- Address: 17 Yeoksam-ro Street, Gangnam-gu, Seoul, South Korea, 06237
- Country of Birth: Spain
- Family: Ex-wife (Bella Agudelo / Birthday: May 10, 1982 / 34 years old / housewife)
  2 sons (David / Birthday: January 16, 2010 / 6 years old and Gabriel / Birthday: January 31, 2013 / 3 years old)

Zhang Wei

- Gender: Male
- Birthday: December 3, 1997
- Age: 19
- Phone number: Home: 02-2879-2537
  Cell: 010-9955-1993
- Address: 147 Yangjae-daero Street, Gangdong-gu, Seoul, South Korea, 05257
- Country of Birth: China
- Family: Single / never been married

Erica Park

- Gender: Female
- Birthday: January 16, 1996
- Age: 20
- Phone number: Cell: 010-9754-7234
- Address: 101-705 Xia Apartment, 13 Sadang-ro Street Seoul, South Korea, 07003
- Address in the US: 1652 Navy Avenue San Diego CA
- Country of Birth: U.S.A.
- Family: Dad (Jason Park / Birthday: December 3, 1967 / 49 years old)
  Mom (Alice Park / Birthday: June 21, 1968 / 48 years old)
  Sister (Jade Park / Birthday: July 8, 2000 / 16 years old)
  Grandpa (Park / Birthday: December 14, 1945 / 71 years old)
  Grandma (Park / Birthday: August 15, 1947 / 69 years old)

UNIT

1 Meetings and Greetings

Warm-up Questions:

(Some of these questions will be a review from Book 1)

1. How are you doing today?

   I'm doing ______________ .

2. How was your vacation?

   It was ______________ .

WHY ARE THESE "BAD"?

"Good" Response		"Bad" Response	
good	not bad	terrible	sad
so-so	fine	bad	lonely
okay	well	hungry	not good
alright	________	wonderful	busy
________	________	________	________

NOTE: People can be "well", but things cannot be "well". Things "go well".

Example:
I **am** doing well. Thank you.
My vacation **is going** well. Thank you.

Common things that "go well":
- first dates / dating
- travelling
- interviews
- your day
- your work
- health procedures (surgery / treatment)

3. What was the best thing you did during the vacation?

The best thing I did during my vacation was ______________________ .

(vacation activity)

Vacation Activities:

- going to the beach
- sleeping in and relaxing
- spending time with family / friends
- taking pictures of beautiful places
- trying new food
- spending time in nature / outdoors
- learning about a new culture

Conversation Corner 1: *Meeting Again*

Getting to know each other. Learning how to ask questions politely.

What's up! It's been a while since I've seen you. What have you been up to?	What's going on? Longtime no see! How have you been?	It is nice to meet you again. Thank you for inviting me a second time.

Hello again, professor.
It is nice to see you again.
Did you have a good summer vacation?

Hello, Mr. Smith.
I hope things have been going well for you.
Did you have a nice summer?

Wow! Look at you!
You look great!
What have you been doing?

Look at the pictures above:

- What do you see?
- Are the people friends?
- Are the pictures of formal or informal situations?

Conversation and Action:

In the pictures, we see different actions, from hugging, shaking hands and waving.
In a group, discuss when you think each action is best.
Remember, this is a cultural issue, so it may change from place to place.

Hugging

- Who: ------------------------
- When: ------------------------

Shaking hands

- Who: ------------------------
- When: ------------------------

Other:

- Fistbump,

------------------------,

------------------------,

------------------------,

------------------------.

- Who: ------------------------
- When: ------------------------

Bowing

- Who: ------------------------
- When: ------------------------

Waving

- Who: ------------------------
- When: ------------------------

Dialogue A: "What have you been up to?"

P.K.:	Hey Marco. How have you been?
Marco:	Hey, P.K.! 1. Is that you? You look so relaxed!
P.K.:	Yeah, the family and I made it to a few beaches over the vacation.
Marco:	Wow. Sounds fantastic.
P.K.:	What about you? How was your vacation? 2. Did you stay out of trouble?
Marco:	You know me. I spent too much time looking for Misses Right, and never really enjoyed my time alone that well. I ought to get hitched like you!
P.K.:	I think you are enjoying single life a bit too much for that. Hold on a second, I think that is Prof. Horeda.
P.K.:	Good afternoon, Prof. Horeda. It is nice to see you again, sir.
Prof. Horeda:	Mr. Olivier, nice to see you. Did you enjoy the vacation?
P.K.:	Yes, sir. 3. It was a good rest. This is Marco. He is a student here as well.
Prof. Horeda:	Nice to meet you, Marco. (shakes hands).
Marco:	It is an honor to meet you, sir,
P.K.:	How about your vacation, sir? 4. Did you do anything special?
Prof. Horeda:	I managed to get to the golf course a few times and hit a few balls. That is all I ever need.
P.K.:	Sounds great, sir.
Prof. Horeda:	Listen, Mr. Olivier, I got to get going but 5. drop by my office sometime and say hi.
P.K.:	Will do, sir. Have a great afternoon.

Substitution Drill: Use the following responses in the above conversation.

		A. FORMAL	B. INFORMAL
1.	Is that you?	I almost didn't recognize you.	You look different. What a surprise!
2.	Did you stay out of trouble?	Do you have any exciting stories?	Did you get into any trouble?
3.	It was a good rest.	I was able to relax and enjoy myself.	I am well rested now.
4.	Did you do anything special?	What interesting things did you do?	Did you do anything of note?
5.	drop by my office sometime	visit my office sometime later	come to my office for a short visit

Grammar Gallery 1: *Present Simple Tense Review*

The present simple is used with frequency adverbs such as "always", "usually", "often", "sometimes", "rarely" and "never". It is also used with every ________ (example: every day / every morning / every Saturday)
It is used mostly for repeated actions (routine, habits) and for general facts (always true).

Pronoun	Affirmative	Negative	Inquisitive?(Question)	
I You We They	play go eat study do drink	don't play don't go don't eat don't study don't do don't drink	Do I play…? Do you go…? Do we eat…? Do they study…? Do I do…? Do you drink…?	Yes, I do. / No, I don't. Yes, you do. / No, you don't. Yes, we do. / No, we don't. Yes, they do. / No, they don't. Yes, I do. / No, I don't. Yes, you do. / No, you don't.
He She It (+S)	plays goes eats studies does drinks	doesn't play doesn't go doesn't eat doesn't study doesn't do doesn't drink	Does he play…? Does she go…? Does it eat…? Does he study…? Does she do…? Does it drink…?	Yes, he does. / No, he doesn't. Yes, she does. / No, she doesn't. Yes, it does. / No, it doesn't. Yes, he does. / No, he doesn't. Yes, she does. / No, she doesn't. Yes, it does. / No, it doesn't.

Exercise 1 *Fill in the blanks with the correct version of the verb:*

1. They ________________ (dance) on Friday nights.
2. She ________________ (go) to school every Monday, Wednesday and Friday.
3. She and I ________________ (like) to eat chicken.
4. Peter is a boxer. He ________________ (box) every morning to keep in shape.
5. We always ________________ (drink) milk in the morning.
6. He usually ________________ (take) the shuttle bus to school.
7. She ________________ (watch) T.V. every Sunday evening.
8. They ________________ (talk) quietly in class.
9. You and your friend ________________ (play) soccer very well.
10. He ________________ (swim) very well.

Exercise 2 *Fill in the blanks with the correct form of the verb in the negative:*

1. They ________________ (not eat) pizza because it is too fattening.
2. He ________________ (not walk) to school. He takes the bus.
3. Bonny ________________ (not go) home after school. She goes to a part-time job.
4. John ________________ (not study) English very hard. He needs to work harder.
5. He ________________ (not drink) alcohol. It makes him feel terrible.
6. They ________________ (not meet) for coffee very often. Both of them are very busy.
7. She ________________ (not need) to go to the gym. She does yoga every morning.
8. The teachers ________________ (not give) too much homework. We should be happy.
9. My favorite teacher ________________ (not speak) quietly in class.
10. It ________________ (not eat) vegetables. It only eats meat.

Exercise 3 *Fill in the blanks with the correct form of the verb in the following questions:*

1. ________________ they ________________ (go) to school here?
2. ________________ he ________________ (work) part-time?
3. How often ________________ Bonny ________________ (practice) the violin?
4. Where ________________ John ________________ (live)? Is it near here?
5. Why ________________ you ________________ (enjoy) shopping so much?
6. When ________________ they ________________ (meet) for coffee?
7. How often ________________ she ________________ (do) yoga?
8. What ________________ the teachers ________________ (like) to do on summer vacation?
9. Where ________________ he ________________ (watch) movies?
10. ________________ you ________________ (want) to watch a movie with me tonight?

Exercise 4 *About you and your partner: Answer the questions below.*

1. What do you always do in the morning?

   I always ______________________ in the morning.

   My partner always ______________________ in the morning.

2. What do you sometimes do on Friday?

   I sometimes ______________________ on Fridays.

   My partner sometimes ______________________ on Fridays.

3. What do you often do during the week?

   I often ______________________ during the week.

   My partner often ______________________ during the week.

4. What do you rarely do?

   I rarely ______________________ .

   My partner rarely ______________________ .

5. What is something you never do?

   I never ______________________ .

   My partner never ______________________ .

Exercise 5 *Use the present simple to complete the following.*

Does he like movies?

____

Does she enjoy kimchi?

____

Where do ducks fly in the winter?

____

How does he feel?

____

Do they play golf?

____

What does the student eat for lunch?

____

What does she do on Sundays?

____

Do we need our passports to go abroad?

____

Do they hike together?

____

Dialogue B: *"Long Time No See."*

Michelle: Erica, is that you?

Erica: Wow, Michelle?

Michelle: Yes! Erica, it has been such a long time. I almost didn't recognize you.

Erica: You, too. You look so different. 1. Long time no see.

Michelle: Where are you going right now? Are you in a hurry?

Erica: Yes, I'm heading to class right now. 2. But I would love to catch up with you. Take a walk with me?

Michelle: I'd love to. When was the last time I saw you? Was it in English Conversation Class for first years?

Erica: Oh my goodness. Has it been that long?

Michelle: I think so. So, what are you up to these days? 3. Seeing anyone special?

Erica: I wish. No boyfriend currently. I work part-time at my father's Korean restaurant and study during the week. Not much to say. What about you?

Michelle: I took a year off after the first year of university to travel and study languages a bit. I travelled around South America and had a lot of fun.

Erica: So you must be very good at Spanish now.

Michelle: 4. I can get by, but I learned more how to cook the food from Brazil and Peru. The food down there is so exotic and savory.

Erica: Wow, sounds great. Listen, I have to go to class now but here is my phone number. 010-3248-2878. Why don't we get together sometime soon?

Michelle: That sounds wonderful. See you soon. 5. We'll catch up more then.

Substitution Drill: Use the following responses in the above conversation.

		A. FORMAL	B. INFORMAL
1.	Long time no see.	It has been a while since we last met.	I haven't seen you for a long time.
2.	But I would love to catch up with you.	But I would like to get to know you again.	But I want to hear about what you have been doing.
3.	Seeing anyone special?	Are you in a relationship?	Are you dating anyone?
4.	I can get by,	I know enough to be comfortable,	I speak enough to survive,
5.	We'll catch up more then.	We can finish learning about each other again.	We can talk more about what we have been doing later.

Grammar Gallery 2: *Present Continuous Review:*

In this example, we are using "play"

Pronoun	Affirmative	Negative	Yes/No Question
I	am (verb)ing *am playing	am not (verb)ing *am not playing	Am I (verb)ing? { Yes, I am. (Yes, you are.) No, I am not. (No, you are not.)
You We They	are (verb)ing *are playing	are not (verb)ing *are not playing *aren't playing	Are you / we / they (verb)ing? { Yes, you are. No, you are not.
He She It	is (verb)ing *is playing	is not (verb)ing *is not playing *isn't playing	Is he / she / it (verb)ing? { Yes, he is. No, he is not.

*To make it easier to remember, say the ➡ AM / IS / ARE ING NOW!
5 times out loud.

Spelling Review:

NOTE: MOST WORDS ARE JUST "+ ING"

Ex. play + ing = playing eat + ing = eating drink + ing = drinking
go + ing = going walk + ing = walking study + ing = studying
read + ing = reading wait + ing = waiting do + ing = doing

Exceptions:

1. Last letter "e" (silent "e"): If the word's last letter is an "e", you can remove the "e" before adding "+ ing".

   Ex. write + ing = writing come + ing = coming bake + ing = baking
   ride + ing = riding hope + ing = hoping make + ing = making
   **Words ending in two "ee"s, just + ing:*
   see + ing = seeing agree + ing = agreeing flee + ing =fleeing

2. For short vowel sound words, you double the last letter.
   SHORT VOWEL SOUND ➡ "a" in apple, "e" in bet, "i" in hit, "o" in lot, "u" in bug

   Ex. run + ing = running jog + ing = jogging swim + ing = swimming

3. Last letters "ie": If the last letters of the word are "ie", then you change "ie" to "y"

   Ex. lie + ing = lying tie + ing = tying die + ing = dying

Exercise 6 *Write the correct "be" verb and the correct "verb"+ing form in the blanks below. Below, write the answer with "not". The first one is done for you.*

1. He / go : He is going. / He is not going. / He isn't going.
2. I / run: ______
3. They / sit: ______
4. You / study: ______
5. She / lie: ______
6. We / joke: ______
7. It / dance: ______
8. He / shop: ______
9. They / ski: ______
10. You / hike: ______
11. We / eat: ______
12. She / take: ______
13. I / squeeze: ______
14. It / die: ______
15. You / see: ______

*We use the present continuous when we are talking about things that are happening now and in the near future.

REMEMBER: You can choose to use the contraction (aren't / isn't) and that is fine but considered "low level" for academic writing.
(축약한 표현(aren't / isn't)을 사용할 수도 있고 문제는 없지만 학술적인 글에서는 수준이 낮은 것으로 간주된다는 것을 기억하세요.)

Exercise 7 *Look at the following pictures and write what is happening using the present continuous.*

1. ______________________

____

2. ______________________

____

3. ______________________

____

4. ______________________

____

5. ______________________

____

6. ______________________

____

7. ______________________

____

8. ______________________

____

9. ______________________

____

Present Continuous Yes / No question Review:

Pronoun	Affirmative	Negative	Yes/No Question			
I	am (verb)ing *am playing	am not (verb)ing *am not playing	Am	I	(verb)ing?	Yes, I am. (Yes, you are.) No, I am not. (No, you are not.)
You We They	are (verb)ing *are playing	are not (verb)ing *are not playing *aren't playing	Are	you we they	(verb)ing?	Yes, you are. No, you are not.
He She It	is (verb)ing *is playing	is not (verb)ing *is not playing *isn't playing	Is	he she it	(verb)ing?	Yes, he is. No, he is not.

REMEMBER: When making questions with the verb "be" involved, the "be" verb usually goes in front of the subject.
("be" 동사를 사용하여 의문문을 만들 때에는 "be" 동사가 주어 앞에 온다는 것을 기억하세요.)

Ex. I am dancing. ➡ Am I dancing?
They are moving. ➡ Are they moving?
You are playing. ➡ Are you playing?
He is drowning. ➡ Is he drowning?

Exercise 8 *Make the statements into questions.*

1. They are walking home.
   Are they walking home?
2. He is playing computer at home.
   ______
3. I am dancing in the rain.
   ______
4. She is walking in the park.
   ______
5. You are cooking fish.
   ______
6. It is running.
   ______
7. George and Sally are eating dinner.
   ______
8. The birds are flying to warmer places.
   ______
9. They are listening to music.
   ______
10. Jonah is watching T.V.
   ______

Exercise 9 *This tense is often used for persons we cannot see (maybe when speaking on the phone) or to talk about things we see in a photograph. Section 1 of TOEIC "Photographs" uses the present continuous very frequently. Answer using the picture. If the answer is "no", please state what is happening in the picture.*

(이 시제는 볼 수 없는 사람을 가리킬 때(전화로 대화할 때와 같이) 또는 사진을 볼 때 종종 사용됩니다. TOEIC의 첫 번째 부분인 "사진묘사" 부분은 현재진행 시제를 매우 빈번히 사용합니다. 사진을 활용하여 대답해 보세요. "NO"라고 대답을 했다면 사진의 내용을 말해보세요.)

Are they walking?

No, they are not.

They are driving a car.

Is she working?

Is he taking a break?

Are they dancing?

Are they staying in tonight?

Are you making dinner now?

Is it sleeping?

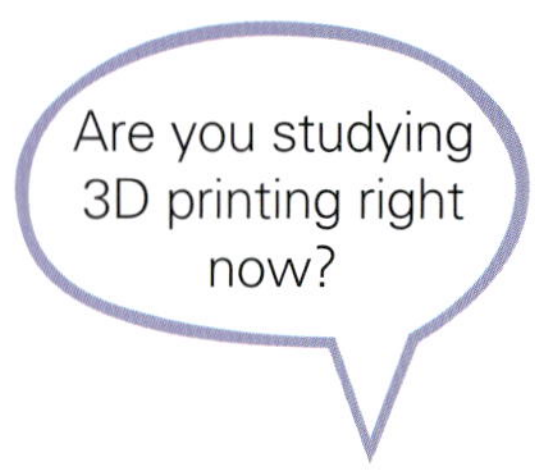

Exercise 10

Present Simple vs. Present Continuous: Putting it all together!
The following sentences contain time words that indicate whether an action is present simple (routine habit) or present continuous. Write the correct form of the verb in the blanks.

1. Now, I ____________ (eat) breakfast. I usually ____________ (eat) breakfast at 8:00 a.m.
2. Now, you ____________ (do) grammar. You often ____________ (do) grammar in English class.
3. She ____________ (brush) her teeth three times a day. She ____________ (brush) her teeth right now.
4. Julianna ____________ (play) soccer now. Julianna ____________ (play) soccer once a week.
5. Frank usually ____________ (watch) T.V. in the evenings. Now, Frank ____________ (not watch) T.V. because he ____________ (get) ready for a date.
6. A lion ____________ (eat) meat. Lions ____________ (not eat) vegetables. Now, the lions ____________ (not eat). The lions ____________ (sleep) now.
7. I ____________ (enjoy) hiking. I ____________ (hike) whenever I have time. Unfortunately, I ____________ (live) in Seoul. There are not many good mountain trails close to where I live.
8. What ____________ I ____________ (do) now? I ____________ (watch) T.V. and ____________ (try) to relax. How about you? What ____________ you ____________ (do)?
9. How often ____________ he ____________ (go) to Busan? He ____________ (go) to Busan about twice a month. I think he ____________ (start) to date someone down there recently.
10. Where ____________ you ____________ (go)? We just started playing the round of cards. I ____________ (take) a quick break. I always ____________ (talk) to my girlfriend at this time. I'll be back soon.

Phrasal Verbs using "GET":

Phrasal Verb	Meaning	Example
Get along	a. not fighting, being peaceful (사이 좋게 지내다.)	a. The children in the class get along well with each other. There are no problems.
Get up	a. to wake up from sleep (잠자리에서 일어나다.)	a. I usually get up around 6:00 a.m.
Get on	a. to enter a big vehicle, such as a train, airplane, boat, or bus. (기차, 비행기, 배, 버스 등 커다란 운송수단에 타다.)	a. Quickly. Get on the boat before it leaves.
Get in	a. to enter a small vehicle, such as a taxi or car. (택시나 승용차 같은 조그만 운송수단에 타다.)	a. I made sure she got in her car before I left her.
Get ready	a. to prepare for something (준비하다.)	a. Did you get ready for the job interview?
Get scared	a. to be frightened (겁먹다.)	a. I get really scared of thriller movies.
Get even	a. to do something to make things balanced (균형을 맞추다.)	a. She said she would get even with her sister for wearing the sweater.
Get out	a. to exit a vehicle, usually small like a taxi or car (택시나 승용차처럼 조그만 운송수단에서 내리다.) b. to go out for fun (즐기기 위해 나가다.)	a. Ok. You can get out of the car now. b. I am working too hard. I need to get out.
Get mad / Get angry	a. to become angry (화나다.)	a. She really got mad when I suggested her boyfriend was a weird guy.

Ask in your group:

- What do you **get ready** for?
- When was the last time you **got mad**?
- When do you usually **get in** a car?
- Who do you **get along** with?
- When do you want to **get even**?
- What time do you **get up**?
- When was the last time you **got scared**?
- What time do you usually **go out** on Saturdays?

TOEIC VOCABULARY

Read the following common TOEIC words. Memorize so that you can do well on the TOEIC. Write the Korean and English in the space below two times to help you learn.

Strategy: 전략.
It is the president's role to develop the overall strategy of the company.
회사의 전반적인 전략을 수립하는 것이 사장의 역할이다.

_______ / _______ _______ / _______

Strictly: 엄격히.
The ban on smoking on the premises of the company is not strictly enforced.
회사 구내에서의 금연의 엄격히 집행되지 않고 있다.

_______ / _______ _______ / _______

Stringent: 엄중한, 절박한.
Stringent anti-noise regulations should be adopted for a better education.
보다 나은 교육을 위해 엄격한 소음규제 규정을 도입해야 한다.

_______ / _______ _______ / _______

Struggle: 노력, 투쟁, 노력하다, 투쟁하다.
There was a power struggle between forces favoring and opposing change.
변화를 선호하는 세력과 반대하는 세력 사이에 권력투쟁이 있었다.

_______ / _______ _______ / _______

Subject to: ~하기 쉬운.
All flights are subject to delay without prior notice.
모든 비행은 사전 통지 없이 연기될 수 있다.

_______ / _______ _______ / _______

Subsequent: 뒤이은.
These skills should be passed on to subsequent generations.
이런 기술은 후대에 전승되어야 한다.

_______ / _______ _______ / _______

Substantial: 상당한.
The current situation requires substantial changes.
현 상황은 상당한 변화를 요구한다.

_______ / _______ _______ / _______

Sufficient: 충분한.
Unauthorized absence is sufficient reason for dismissal in every company.
무단 결근은 모든 회사에서 해고의 충분한 사유가 된다.

_______ / _______ _______ / _______

Suitable: 적합한.
The house is not really suitable for a large family.
이 집은 대가족에게는 정말 적합하지 않다.

_______ / _______ _______ / _______

Supplement: 보충, 보충물.
Every morning, I take vitamins and other dietary supplements.
매일 아침 비타민과 다른 식이용 보충식품을 섭취한다.

_______ / _______ _______ / _______

Surplus: 잉여의.
Surplus cash can be invested for the future.
잉여 현금은 미래를 위해 투자할 수 있다.

_______ / _______ _______ / _______

Sustain: 지탱하다, 버티다, 당하다.
The company has sustained heavy financial losses this year.
우리 회사는 올해 상당한 재정 손실을 입었다.

_______ / _______ _______ / _______

Tailor: 맞추다.
Treatment is tailored to the needs of each patient.
치료는 환자 개개인의 필요에 맞추어진다.

_______ / _______ _______ / _______

Tariff: 관세.
Every country imposes tariffs on imported goods.
모든 나라는 수입품에 관세를 부과한다.

_______ / _______ _______ / _______

Tentative: 임시의.
The government is taking tentative steps towards tackling the country's economic problems.

정부는 국가의 경제 문제를 해결하기 위한 임시 조치를 취하고 있다.

_________ / _________ _________ / _________

Thoroughly: 철저히.
The screening of applicants must be done thoroughly.
지원자 전형은 철저하게 해야 한다.

_________ / _________ _________ / _________

Timely: 시의 적절한.
We aim to settle all valid claims in a timely manner.
모든 타당한 요구를 제 때에 처리하려고 한다.

_________ / _________ _________ / _________

Transaction: 거래.
The bank charges a fixed rate for each transaction.
은행은 모든 거래에 고정된 요금을 부과한다.

_________ / _________ _________ / _________

Tremendous: 거대한, 엄청난.
She praised her husband for the tremendous support he had given her.
그녀는 남편이 자기에게 준 커다란 지원 때문에 남편을 칭찬했다.

_________ / _________ _________ / _________

Typically: 전형적으로.
In the animal kingdom, the male is typically smaller than the female.
동물세계에서 수컷이 항상 암컷보다 작다.

_________ / _________ _________ / _________

Ultimately: 궁극적으로.
He has finished a long but ultimately successful election campaign.
그는 오래 되었지만 결국 성공적인 선거 유세를 마쳤다.

_________ / _________ _________ / _________

Unprecedented: 전례가 없는.
The export of cars has increased on an unprecedented scale.
승용차 수출이 전례 없는 규모로 증가하였다.

_________ / _________ _________ / _________

Upon request: 요청에 따라.
Further details will be sent upon request.
추가 사항은 요청하시면 드립니다.

_________ / _________ _________ / _________

Vacate: 비우다.
In many cases, hotel guests must vacate their rooms by noon.
많은 경우 호텔 투숙객들은 정오까지는 방을 비워야 한다.

_________ / _________ _________ / _________

Vary: 다양하다.
Charges vary according to size.
요금은 크기에 따라 다릅니다.

_________ / _________ _________ / _________

Verify: 증명하다, 검증하다.
Peace Corps will remain to verify compliance with the armistice treaty.
평화유지군은 휴전 조약 준수를 검증하기 위해 잔류할 것이다.

_________ / _________ _________ / _________

Violate: 위반하다, 침해하다.
The mass media has a tendency to violate people's privacy.
대중 매체는 사람들의 사생활을 침해하는 경향이 있다.

_________ / _________ _________ / _________

Wage: 임금.
In some business areas, women receive lower wages than men.
일부 사업 영역에서 여성이 남성보다 낮은 임금을 받는다.

_________ / _________ _________ / _________

Waive: 포기하다, 철회하다.
She waived her right to a lawyer.
그녀는 변호사에게 권리를 위임했다.

_________ / _________ _________ / _________

Wallet: 지갑.
He took some cash out of his wallet.
그는 지갑에서 현금을 좀 꺼냈다.

_________ / _________ _________ / _________

UNIT 2 Where Were You Last Night?

Review Questions:

1. How was your vacation?

   It was ______________________ .

2. What was the best thing you did during the vacation?

   The best thing I did during my vacation was ______________________ .

Warm-up Questions:

4. When is your birthday?

   My birthday is in ______________________ .
   (month)

   My birthday is on ______________________ .
   (month day)

5. Where did you celebrate your last birthday party?

   I celebrated my last birthday party at ______________ .
   (place)

In a group, brainstorm places to celebrate birthdays.

- at home
- ______________________
- ______________________
- ______________________

6. What presents did you get from your friends and family?

   I got ______________ for my birthday.
   (gifts / presents)

Months of the Year

1 – January
2 – February
3 – March
4 – April
5 – May
6 – June
7 – July
8 – August
9 – September
10 – October
11 – November
12 – December

Common Birthday Gifts.

– flowers
– clothes
– chocolates
– cell phones / cell phone accessories
– jewelry

Dialogue A: *"How was your birthday?"*

Michelle: Hey Tiffiny. How was your weekend?

Tiffiny: Hi, Michelle. 1. It was awesome! How about your weekend?

Michelle: Well, 2. your weekend sounds way more exciting than mine. I just studied English and watched some movies. What did you do?

Tiffiny: It was my birthday last week on Wednesday. So on Saturday night I had a party with my friends, then on Sunday I had lunch with my family.

Michelle: That sounds great! Where did you have your birthday party?

Tiffiny: First, we went to a BBQ restaurant near Seoul Station. Then we went to a karaoke bar. 3. We had a lot to drink, then sang and danced until late. It was super fun!

Michelle: Oh, I love karaoke bars! Where did you have lunch with your family?

Tiffiny: We had lunch at home. We ordered my favorite food… pizza! Then we had a Baskin Robbins ice cream cake. 4. I ate way too much!

Michelle: Did you get any presents?

Tiffiny: I did! My friends got me a handbag and my parents got me a new cell phone. Check it out!

Michelle: 5. I'm so jealous! I can't wait for my birthday.

Tiffiny: When is that?

Michelle: Not for another 5 months. It is in July.

Tiffiny: Remind me and I'll get you something.

Substitution Drill: Use the following responses in the above conversation.

		A. FORMAL	B. INFORMAL
1.	It was awesome!	My weekend was quite good. Thank you!	It was so good!
2.	your weekend sounds way more exciting	it sounds like your weekend was far better than mine	your weekend sounds much more interesting
3.	We had a lot to drink, then sang and danced until late.	We managed to spend the whole time enjoying food, drinks and song.	We had some laughs and had a great time.
4.	I ate way too much!	I ate more than I should have.	I really pigged out!
5.	I'm so jealous!	I envy your wonderful party.	I wish my weekend was just as exciting as yours was.

Conversation Corner: Asking About Occupations

As shown in previous exercises and book 1, there are many ways to say the same thing, but some are used in more formal and informal situations.

First, let's collect a list of uncommon jobs for you and your group to find the Korean:

• secretary:	• performer:
• electrician:	• athlete:
• plumber:	• judge:
• chef:	• shopkeeper:
• manager:	• custodian:
• nursing aide:	• landscaper:

Ways of asking about occupations: As a class, add more ways of asking this question; then practice with a partner.

FORMAL	INFORMAL
• May I ask what you do?	• What do you do?
• May I ask what you do for a living?	• What is your job?
• Could I ask what your occupation is?	• What is your 9 to 5?
• Could I ask what your job is?	• Where do you work?
• May I ask where you are employed?	• Who do you work for?
	• What do you do these days?
______________________	______________________
______________________	______________________
______________________	______________________
______________________	

CULTURAL NOTE: NOT HAVING A JOB!
There are also many ways that you can say that you don't have a job.
Here are two good ways to say the same.
"I am currently unemployed at the moment."
"I am between jobs right now."

With your partner, practice the above and ask about jobs.
*아르바이트 is German, not English

- May I ask what your job is? I'm a ______________ (job title). / I work at ______________ (job place).

  I'm a part-time ______________ (job title). / I work part-time at ______________ (job place).

- May I ask what your father does? My father is a ______________ (job title).

  My father works at ______________ (job place).

- May I ask what your mother does? My mother is a ______________ (job title).

  My mother works at ______________ (job place).

Grammar Gallery 1: *Past tense of verb "be" using "was" or "were"*

Subject	Past tense affirmative	Possible answer
I	was	happy.
You	were	late for school.
We	were	busy.
They	were	on vacation.
He	was	at home.
She	was	tired.
It	was	cold and rainy.
Name (Sue / John)	was	born in Spain.

Exercise 1 *Past tense of "be": Use the grammar chart above to complete the following exercises.*

1. He ______________ tired.
2. Susan ______________ single until 29 years old.
3. They ______________ at the cinema.

4. They ________________ funny yesterday.
5. Jenny ________________ sad after the movie.
6. We ________________ in the same class last year.
7. It ________________ hot yesterday.
8. You and I ________________ born in Seoul.
9. I ________________ in bed at 10 p.m.
10. Frank and John ________________ baseball players.
11. Shaun ________________ in his car.
12. The cellphones ________________ off during class.
13. We ________________ ready to study.
14. We ________________ angry.
15. You ________________ at the beach last weekend.
16. John ________________ a teacher.
17. The night ________________ dark and spooky.
18. They ________________ unhappy.
19. I ________________ being sarcastic.
20. The students ________________ tired.

Exercise 2 *Make your own sentences using "was" or "were" to complete the sentences. You need to add the "in", "on" or "at" if necessary.*

1. (The dog / bathroom / yesterday)

____

2. (The pirates / boat / last weekend)

____

	3. (The elephant / ball / at last night's circus performance) ______________________________________
	4. (He / on vacation / beach / last summer) ______________________________________
	5. (She / sad yesterday because she dropped her ice cream) ______________________________________
	6. (4th grade boys / shorter than the girls) ______________________________________

Exercise 3 *Listening: Read the short story about Jake and Leena's vacation. Fill in the blanks with "was" or "were".*

Last week we ________ on vacation. Jake ________ very happy because we went to his favorite place… the beach! The weather ________ beautiful. The water ________ quite cool, but we still went swimming. The hotel ________ very big! It had 100 rooms. Our room ________ very luxurious. I ________ pleased because we had an amazing view of the ocean. There were many tourists at our hotel. They ________ from lots of different countries. We met Ashley and George. They ________ from Thailand and they ______ very friendly. On our last night, we attended a show. It ______ amazing! We saw a traditional dance. The costumes ______ fantastic. There ______ also elephants in the performance. Jack ______ excited because he loves elephants. What a great vacation!

Exercise 4 *Answer the questions from the story about Jack's vacation.*

Part 1: Find the answer:

1. How was the water at the beach?

______.

2. How did Jack feel when he was on vacation?

______.

3. Where were the other tourists from?

______.

4. What animals were in the performance?

______.

Part 2: Inference: Find the answer from understanding:

1. How old do you think Jack is? Why?

______.

2. What country do you think Jack went to? Why?

______.

Dialogue B: *"When I was a young boy..."*

Wei: I didn't know you played the guitar! I saw a photo on your Facebook page of you playing the guitar.

Marco: Yeah, 1. I started playing a few years ago. When I was young, I played the piano. But I wasn't really very excited by it. I always wanted to play the guitar though. How about yourself? Do you play any instruments?

Wei: No, not now. When I was at elementary school, I also played the piano. 2. But I stopped when I went to middle school. There wasn't enough time for everything.

Marco: Yeah, 3. as we get older we get so busy. It's sad to stop doing things because we have no time anymore. What else did you do when you were young?

Wei: My family used to spend summer vacation 4. at the beach. My Dad was really keen on camping. He was so happy and stress-free on those vacations. I made many friends camping. They were close friends but we lost touch over the years. How about you?

Marco: When I was young, 5. my family was crazy about hiking. My parents were excited to find new mountains to hike. I remember driving all over on our vacations to visit new mountains.

Wei: And now, all our free time is for studying and working! I wish I were a kid again!

Marco: Me too. I was happier then!

Substitution Drill: Use the following responses in the above conversation.

		A. FORMAL	B. INFORMAL
1.	I started playing a few years ago.	I decided to start learning a few years ago.	I picked it up a couple years ago.
2.	But I stopped when I went to middle school.	But as I got busy in middle school, I was forced to give it up.	I had to quit when I got to middle school.
3.	as we get older we get so busy.	it always gets busier as life moves on.	we are less free every day.
4.	at the beach.	near the seaside.	on the sands at the seashore.
5.	my family was crazy about hiking.	we loved hiking together as a family.	my family really enjoyed hiking.

Grammar Gallery 2: *Past tense of "be"*

– negative with contractions and short questions and answers.

Negative with 'not'

Subject	Past tense negative	Past tense negative with contraction	possible answer
I	was not →	wasn't	happy.
You	were not →	weren't	late for school.
We	were not →	weren't	busy.
They	were not →	weren't	on vacation.
He	was not →	wasn't	at home.
She	was not →	wasn't	tired.
It	was not →	wasn't	cold and rainy.
Name (Sue / John)	was not →	wasn't	born in Korea.

REMEMBER THE RULE: When making questions from a statement with the verb "be", move the verb "be" in front of the subject, which can include other words.
(기억해야 할 규칙: 평서문을 바탕으로 "be" 동사를 가지고 의문문을 만들 때에는 "be" 동사를 주어 앞에 두어야 하며 주어는 다른 단어도 포함할 수 있습니다.)

- He *was* hungry. ➡ *Was* he hungry?
- The children *were* playing a game. ➡ What *were* the children playing?

Short answer questions

Question	Affirmative	Negative
Was I happy?	Yes, I was.	No, I wasn't.
Were you late for school?	Yes, you were.	No, you weren't.
Were we busy?	Yes, we were.	No, we weren't.
Were they on vacation?	Yes, they were.	No, they weren't.
Was he at home?	Yes, he was.	No, he wasn't
Was she tired?	Yes, she was.	No, she wasn't.
Was it cold and rainy?	Yes, it was.	No, it wasn't.
Was Sue late?	Yes, she was.	No, she wasn't.
Was John born in Korea?	Yes, he was.	No, he wasn't.

Exercise 5 *Negative past tense of "be" with contractions.*
Choose the correct past tense "be" verb "was", "were", "wasn't" or "weren't" to complete the sentences.

1. They __________ in Los Angeles.
2. __________ you home late last night? Yes, I __________ .
3. __________ Mike at work yesterday? Yes, he __________ .
4. She __________ at school.
5. __________ they up early this morning? No, they __________ .
6. I __________ angry.
7. Rachel __________ in bed.
8. __________ we hungry? Yes, we __________ .
9. __________ Megan on the bus this morning? No, she __________ .
10. We __________ on the bus.
11. He __________ in the park.
12. __________ he happy to see you? No, he __________ .
13. __________ it busy in Seoul at Chuseok? Yes, it __________ .
14. It __________ an interesting movie.

Exercise 6 *Make one affirmative and one negative sentence using the past tense of "be": "was" "wasn't" "were", "weren't".*

Example: London is a good city. London was a good city. London wasn't a good city.

1. He is a smart student. __________ . __________ .
2. It is hot. __________ . __________ .
3. They are clever. __________ . __________ .
4. Mary is rich. __________ . __________ .
5. We are cold. __________ . __________ .
6. Andrew is silly. __________ . __________ .
7. You are excited. __________ . __________ .
8. She is beautiful. __________ . __________ .

Exercise 7 *Change the sentences to the past tense. Then make a short question.*

Example: Bob is funny. Bob was funny. Was Bob funny?

1. They are on holiday. ______________. ______________?
2. You are sick. ______________. ______________?
3. She is in Australia. ______________. ______________?
4. Joe is from Germany. ______________. ______________?
5. I am smart. ______________. ______________?
6. We are young. ______________. ______________?
7. He is strong. ______________. ______________?
8. Melissa is old. ______________. ______________?

Exercise 8 *Group conversation / Speaking practice:*
Take turns to ask and answer questions with your partner.

QUESTION	PARTNER'S RESPONSE
Were you a good student in high school?	
Was it rainy yesterday?	
Was your dad handsome when he was young?	
Were your friends drinking alcohol last night?	
Was your house near your elementary school?	
Were your grandparents alive when you were born?	
Was your (sister / brother) kind to you when you were little?	

Phrasal Verbs using "TAKE":

Look at the following meanings and example sentences. Ask your teacher for help to understand. Then use the "phrasal verbs" in the blanks below.

Phrasal Verb	Meaning	Example
Take a break	**a.** To have a short rest time. (잠시 쉬다)	**a.** She takes a break at 10:45 a.m.
Take off	**a.** To leave or depart from a place. (떠나다) **b.** To become airborne on a plane. (이륙하다) **c.** To remove an item of clothing. (옷을 벗다)	**a.** I'm taking off now. Good night! **b.** The plane takes off at 6:15. Be at the airport at least two hours before then. **c.** He takes off his hat in the classroom.
Take out	**a.** When you buy food at a restaurant, then eat it somewhere else. (나가서 먹다)	**a.** Would you like to eat in or take out?
Take in	**a.** To include something. (포함하다) **b.** To look at something. (보다) **c.** To understand and remember something. (이해하다, 기억하다)	**a.** My friend took in a stray cat. **b.** I just want to take in the view. **c.** Did you understand the lecture? Yes, I took it all in.
Take up	**a.** To start something. (시작하다)	**a.** He took up pottery after seeing all the women in the class.
Take on	**a.** To begin to do or deal with a new task. (착수하다) **b.** To contend with an opponent in a fight. (싸우다)	**a.** I need to take on more part-time work. I really need the money. **b.** He took on the mugger and was hurt.
Take after	**a.** To resemble someone. (닮다)	**a.** He takes after his father. They act the same.
Take to	**a.** To start liking something. (좋아하게 되다)	**a.** I'm really taking to university life. It's great.

Practice: Finish the sentences using the "take" phrasal verbs.

1. She is really starting to ______________ swimming! She only just started it, but she loves it already.
2. As we stood on the top of the mountain, the view was a lot to ______________ . It was a beautiful sight.
3. I need a new hobby. I think I will ______________ skiing this winter.
4. Can we please ______________ ? My head is hurting from too much studying.
5. He ______________ his father. They look so similar.
6. What time will you ______________ tomorrow? I will leave at the same time.
7. I feel so stressed at work. My boss asked me to ______________ a new project and I couldn't say no.
8. I'm too tired to cook tonight. Let's order ______________ .

TOEIC VOCABULARY

Read the following common TOEIC words. Memorize so that you can do well on the TOEIC. Write the Korean and English in the space below two times to help you learn.

Remit: 송금하다.
Please remit the instalment payment by check or mail order.
수표 또는 우편환으로 할부금을 보내 주십시오.

_________ / _________ _________ / _________

Renovation: 혁신, 개혁, 수리.
The renovation work for the hotel will take at least 3 months.
호텔 개축 공사는 최소한 3개월 걸릴 것이다.

_________ / _________ _________ / _________

Repetitive: 반복적인.
House chores include repetitive tasks like washing and ironing.
집안 일은 빨래와 다림질 같은 반복적 일이 포함된다.

_________ / _________ _________ / _________

Replacement: 대체물, 대체 근무자.
It was difficult to find a replacement for him.
그 사람을 대체할 수 있는 인력을 찾기가 힘들다.

_________ / _________ _________ / _________

Reserve: 예약하다.
Do you have to reserve tickets in advance?
입장권을 미리 예약해야 합니까?

_________ / _________ _________ / _________

Residential: 거주의.
The elderly prefer a quiet residential neighborhood.
노년층은 조용한 거주 지역을 선호한다.

_________ / _________ _________ / _________

Resolve: 해결하다.
The crisis should be resolved by negotiations.
이번 위기는 협상을 하여 해결해야 한다.

_________ / _________ _________ / _________

Respective: 각각의, 개별적인.
We all went back to our respective homes to wait for news.
우리 모두는 각자 집으로 돌아가서 뉴스를 기다렸다.

_________ / _________ _________ / _________

Restore: 회복하다.
Her parents hoped that the Balkan climate would restore her to full health.
그녀의 부모는 발칸 지역의 기후가 그녀를 온전하게 회복시켜 줄 것을 바랬다.

_________ / _________ _________ / _________

Restrict: 제한하다.
You may need to restrict public access to certain files.
일부 파일은 대중의 접근을 제한해야 할 필요가 있을 수도 있다.

_________ / _________ _________ / _________

Retain: 보유하다.
The state government wants to retain control of dairy products import.
주 정부는 낙농 제품의 수입 통제권을 보유하고 싶어한다.

_________ / _________ _________ / _________

Revenue: 수입, 세수.
The overall revenue has fallen to the level of $10 million due to frequent strikes.
잦은 파업 때문에 전체 세수가 천만 달러 수준으로 하락했다.

_________ / _________ _________ / _________

Reverse: 역류하다, 파기하다, 뒤집다, 전환, 거꾸로인.
The decision was reversed again for the opposition of many lawyers.
이번 결정은 많은 변호사들의 반대 때문에 다시 뒤집어졌다.

_________ / _________ _________ / _________

Revision: 개정, 복습.
I haven't done enough revision for tomorrow's exam.
내일 시험 대비하여 복습을 충분히 하지 못했다.

_________ / _________ _________ / _________

Reward: 보상, 대가.
The school has a system of rewards and punishments to encourage good behavior.
학교 측은 선행을 장려하기 위해 당근과 채찍 제도를 운용하고 있다.

________ / ________ ________ / ________

Safeguard: 보호하다.
The industry has a duty to safeguard the interests of consumers.
산업계는 소비자의 권익을 보호할 의무가 있다.

________ / ________ ________ / ________

Sales figures: 판매 수치.
The company no longer releases its quarterly sales figures.
회사 측은 더 이상 분기별 판매 수치를 발표하지 않는다.

________ / ________ ________ / ________

Screen: 검토하다, 전형하다.
Your application documents are to be screened by the personnel department.
당신의 지원 서류는 인사과가 검토하게 되어 있습니다.

________ / ________ ________ / ________

Secure: 안전한, 확실한.
It has become difficult to find secure jobs these days.
요즘 안전한 직업을 구하는 것이 힘들어졌다.

________ / ________ ________ / ________

Significant: 중요한, 상당한, 의미 있는.
A significant number of young drivers fail to keep to speed limits.
상당한 수의 젊은 운전자들은 제한 속도를 지키지 않는다.

________ / ________ ________ / ________

Simultaneous: 동시의.
Up to thirty users can have simultaneous access to the system.
최대 30명의 사용자가 동시에 시스템에 접속할 수 있다.

________ / ________ ________ / ________

Slightly: 약간.
The productivity of veteran workers is slightly higher than that of new recruits.
고참 근로자들의 생산성이 신입 직원들의 생산성보다 약간 높다.

________ / ________ ________ / ________

Solely: 유일하게.
Scholarships are given solely on the basis of financial need.
장학금은 재정적인 필요에 기초해서만 주어진다.

________ / ________ ________ / ________

Solicit: 간청하다, 애걸하다, 유혹하다.
She was accused of illegally soliciting campaign contributions.
그녀는 불법적으로 선거자금 기부를 요청하여 기소되었다.

________ / ________ ________ / ________

Solid: 고체의, 견고한.
The device can detect the presence of any solid objects in the water.
그 장비는 수중의 모든 고체 상태 물체의 존재를 추적할 수 있다.

________ / ________ ________ / ________

Somewhat: 약간, 다소.
Things have changed somewhat since then.
그 때 이후로 상황이 다소 변화하였다.

________ / ________ ________ / ________

Specific: 특정한.
He has made several games suitable for specific age groups.
그는 특정 연령대에 적합한 몇 개 게임을 만들었다.

________ / ________ ________ / ________

Speculation: 추정, 투기.
The witness's statement was pure speculation at best.
증인의 진술은 기껏해야 단순한 추정에 불과했다.

________ / ________ ________ / ________

Stability: 안정.
The new army base could threaten the peace and stability of the region.
새로운 군사기지는 지역의 평화와 안정을 위협할 수도 있다.

________ / ________ ________ / ________

Status: 지위, 상태.
These documents have no legal status in Korea.
이런 서류는 한국에서는 어떤 법적인 지위도 지니지 못한다.

________ / ________ ________ / ________

UNIT

3 What We Did Last Week

Review Questions:

1. When is your birthday?

____.

2. Where did you have your birthday party?

____.

3. What presents did you get from your friends and family?

____.

Warm-up Questions:

What is your hobby?

- Hobby (취미):

– Something you enjoy doing

(당신이 즐겨 하는 것)

– Something you do in your free time

(당신이 한가할 때 하는 것)

7. What is your hobby?

My hobby is ______________________.
(verb + ing)

8. What do you enjoy doing?

I enjoy ______________________.
(verb + ing)

9. What do you dislike doing?

I dislike ______________________.
(verb + ing)

Here are some common verbs that need a gerund to follow:

- love (verb)ing
- like (verb)ing
- enjoy (verb)ing
- suggest (verb)ing
- quit (verb)ing
- hate (verb)ing
- practice (verb)ing
- mind (verb)ing
- dislike (verb)ing
- recommend (verb)ing

GRAMMAR NOTE: In today's warm-up questions, we see a double verb pattern ➡ "enjoy (verb)ing" "dislike (verb)ing". After some verbs, the next verb must have "ing". These are called "Gerunds" (동명사).

Dialogue A: *"What do you do these days?"*

Wei: 1. What do you do these days, Erica?
Erica: I am a student and I work part-time at a clothing store.
Wei: Do you have a hobby?
Erica: I enjoy shopping in my free time. How about you?
Wei: Me? Do I enjoy shopping? 2. I'm not a fan of shopping.
Erica: Ha ha ha! No, I mean, what is your hobby, Wei?
Wei: I like watching movies and playing video games. I also like cooking at home.
Erica: 3. Really? I enjoy cooking, too! Well, I actually like baking.
Wei: What can you bake?
Erica: I can bake pies, cakes, cookies, muffins… I baked a blueberry banana bread yesterday.
Wei: Stop! You're making me hungry!
Erica: What about you, Wei? What can you cook?
Wei: I like making pasta, salads, curries…
Erica: Curries? Like Indian curry?
Wei: Sure! 4. I cooked curry last night!
Erica: I love curry! Maybe I can try it someday.
Wei: Well then, how about dinner tomorrow at my place? Can we say 7ish?
Erica: 5. I think that works for me. I'll bake dessert!
Wei: Cool! It's a date.
Erica: See you tomorrow!

Substitution Drill: Use the following responses in the above conversation.

		A. FORMAL	B. INFORMAL
1.	What do you do these days,	What kinds of things have you been doing these days,	What are you up to these days,
2.	I'm not a fan of	I dislike	I don't enjoy
3.	Really?	What a coincidence!	Is that for real?
4.	I cooked curry last night!	I made a nice authentic curry only yesterday!	I just made some last night!
5.	I think that works for me.	I think that I can make that.	7 o'clock sounds good to me.

CULTURAL NOTE:

A. When Wei claims that he doesn't like shopping, Erica laughs and says "No, I mean..." In Korean, this can be translated as

"아니, 내 말은…" (Wei가 장보기를 싫어한다고 말할 때 Erica가 웃으며 말한 "No, I mean…"은 "아니 내 말은…" 이라고 번역할 수 있습니다.)

B. Putting the suffix "ish" behind a time implies that the time is approximate. This is a slang commonly used in American English.

(시간 뒤에 접미사 "ish"를 첨가하면 대략적인 시간을 의미합니다. 미국 영어에서 흔히 사용되는 속어 표현입니다.)

Dialogue Comprehension Questions: Answer in complete sentences.

1. What does Erica enjoy doing in her free time?

____.

2. What can Wei cook?

____.

3. Does Erica like curry?

____.

Conversation Corner: *A Polite Inquiry*

Getting to know each other. Learning how to ask questions politely.

May I ask...? Is it okay if I ask...? Is it all right if...?

Sometimes it may be appropriate to ask a person for permission before asking. This is especially the case if you are not familiar with the person yet and you want to ask something that may be too personal. Using these questions for permission before you ask the question can avoid embarrassing situations. In Korean, this is synonymous to saying

"실례가 안 된다면…" 또는 "…을 물어봐도 괜찮을까요?"

(때로는 질문을 하기 전에 허락을 구하는 것이 적절할 수도 있습니다. 특히 상대방을 아직 잘 모른다거나 지나치게 개인적인 수도 있는 질문을 할 때 그렇게 해야 합니다. 질문을 하기 전에 허락을 구하기 위한 이러한 질문을 활용하면 당황스러운 상황을 피할 수 있습니다. "실례가 안 된다면…" 이나 "…을 물어봐도 괜찮을까요?"라는 한국어 표현과 같은 의미입니다.)

How old are you? ✘ ➡ May I ask how old you are? ✔

The word "may" is more polite than "can" and it is often used to ask questions in a polite and formal manner.

("may"는 "can"보다 정중한 표현이며 정중하게 격식을 갖추어 질문을 할 때 자주 사용됩니다.)

- Can I use this? (casual)
- Yes, you can. (casual)
- May I use this? (polite)
- Yes, you may. (polite)

You can also use the questions "Is it okay if I ask...?" or "Is it all right if I ask...?" "Okay" and "all right" mean the same thing. Using the clause "if I ask" means that you are only proposing to ask the question.
(또한 "Is it okay if I ask ...?" 또는 "Is it all right if I ask ... ?"와 같은 질문을 할 수도 있습니다. "Okay"와 "all right"은 같은 의미입니다. "if I ask"와 같은 절을 사용하는 것은 당신이 질문을 하려고 한다는 것을 의미합니다.)

- "If I ask" in Korean is "물어봐도"
- "Is it okay?" in Korean is "괜찮습니까?"
- "Is it okay if I ask..." in Korean then literally means "…라고 물어봐도 괜찮을까요?"

Practice with a partner:
Ask sensitive information of another person using the polite question form.

(상대방과 연습하기: 정중한 의문문을 사용하여 다른 사람에게 민감한 정보를 물어보세요.)

	QUESTION	POLITE FORM
1.	if your partner has a boyfriend or a girlfriend	Is it okay if I ask if you have a girlfriend?
2.	if your partner has ever failed a class	
3.	if you can use your partner's cell phone	
4.	if you can use your partner's personal things (make-up / hair pin / cigarette etc.)	
5.	if your partner has known anyone who has died	

Grammar Gallery 1: *Past Simple Regular Verbs*

RULE #1: The rule for making verbs into past tense is to add "ed".

Present Tense (원형동사)	Past Tense (과거형동사)	Pronunciation of the -ed
ask	asked	/ t /
cook	cooked	/ t /
miss	missed	/ t /
need	needed	/ id /

RULE #2: If a verb ends with an "e", just add "d" to the end of the word.

Present Tense (원형동사)	Past Tense (과거형동사)	Pronunciation of the -ed
bake	baked	/ t /
like	liked	/ t /
exercise	exercised	/ d /
share	shared	/ d /

RULE #3: If a verb ends with a "short vowel" and "consonant", you double the consonant and add the "ed".

Present Tense (원형동사)	Past Tense (과거형동사)	Pronunciation of the -ed
hug	hugged	/ d /
jog	jogged	/ d /
shop	shopped	/ t /
stop	stopped	/ t /

RULE #4: For verbs that end with a "consonant" and a "y", you must take out the "y" and add an "ied".

Present Tense (원형동사)	Past Tense (과거형동사)	Pronunciation of the -ed
study	studied	/ d /
carry	carried	/ d /
marry	married	/ d /

RULE #5: For some verbs that end with a "vowel" (a e i o u) and then "y", you keep the "y" and add "– ed".

Present Tense (원형동사)	Past Tense (과거형동사)	Pronunciation of the -ed
play	played	/ d /
stay	stayed	/ d /
enjoy	enjoyed	/ d /

PHONEMES OF "– ED"

RULE #1: If the word ends in: "t" or "d" ➡ / id / sound	need ➡ needed (need / id) want ➡ wanted (want / id)
RULE #2: If the word ends in: "s", "sh", "ch", "k", "p", "f" ➡ / t / sound	kiss ➡ kissed (kiss / t) finish ➡ finished (finish / t) punch ➡ punched (punch / t) ask ➡ asked (ask / t) jump ➡ jumped (jump / t) laugh ➡ laughed (laugh / t)
RULE #3: Everything else ➡ / d / sound	stay ➡ stayed (stay / d) jog ➡ jogged (jog / d) study ➡ studied (study / d) escape ➡ escaped (escape / d)

Exercise 1 *Put the verb provided into the past tense. Make sure to use the correct spelling!*

BASE VERB	KOREAN	PAST VERB	BASE VERB	KOREAN	PAST VERB
accept	받아들이다	accepted	move		
add			obey		
agree			offer		
bake			pray		
borrow			punch		
change			relax		
cheer			remember		
copy			reply		
cry			rub		
dance			start		
destroy			study		

Exercise 2 *Complete the sentences. Use the simple past tense form.*

1. I ______________ (miss) the bus this morning.
2. Yesterday, my cousin ______________ (play) the piano in a recital.
3. The day before yesterday, we ______________ (try) a new Thai restaurant.
4. Last week, they ______________ (shop) for clothes at the new mall.
5. Last weekend, I just ______________ (stay) home.
6. Last month, Paul and Jane ______________ (decide) to get married.
7. Last summer, we ______________ (visit) our friends in Hawaii.
8. Last year, she ______________ (work) at a dental clinic.
9. Last night, my family ______________ (watch) a movie at the theatre.
10. Last Friday, he ______________ (ask) me out on a date.
11. A few days ago, a famous chef ______________ (cook) a special dinner for us.

Exercise 3 *Fill in the blanks with the past tense verb.*

The Road Trip

Last summer, my best friend ______________ (ask) me to visit her hometown in California with her. I ______________ (agree) to go, and I ______________ (offer) to drive. We ______________ (plan) which course to take, and we ______________ (rent) a small car. I ______________ (pack) sunglasses, a bikini and lots of sunscreen.

We ______________ (stop) at rest areas and ______________ (use) the bathrooms. We ______________ (visit) a strange museum on the way and ______________ (purchase) some interesting souvenirs in the gift shop. At night, we ______________ (park) our car and ______________ (watch) the stars. We ______________ (talk) about our childhood memories and ______________ (listen) and ______________ (dance) to old 80's dance songs.

When we ______________ (arrive) at her old house, her parents and her dog ______________ (welcome) us. We ______________ (stay) in her old room and ______________ (look) at old family photographs together. Her dad ______________ (grill) us hamburgers on the patio and her mom ______________ (serve) us cold lemonades.

The days ______________ (pass) by quickly. We ______________ (play) catch with her dog and ______________ (hike) up the hill in her backyard. We ______________ (tour) the shops in her neighborhood, and I ______________ (shop) for gifts to bring back home.

In the mornings, we ______________ (jog) down to the beach and ______________ (lounge) in the sun all day. In the evenings, we ______________ (enjoy) the beautiful California sunsets. We ______________ (wish) the trip would never end.

We ______________ (decide) to stay one more day. My best friend ______________ (cry) a little when she ______________ (hug) her parents goodbye. Her dog ______________ (whine) as we ______________ (load) our bags into the trunk. Her parents ______________ (invite) me to come back to relax any time, and I ______________ (thank) them for everything. We ______________ (wave) goodbye until we couldn't see them anymore.

Exercise 4 *Reread the passage above in exercise #2. Categorize the pronunciation of the "ed" phoneme. Fill out the chart below.*

/ d /	/ t /	/ id /
agree	asked	rented

Dialogue B: *"Having a bad day"*

Wei: Erica, come in.
Erica: Thanks, Wei. Sorry, I'm late.
Wei: 1. What's wrong? You look stressed out.
Erica: It's a long story.
Wei: Did you have a bad day?
Erica: I had a very bad day.
Wei: 2. What happened?
Erica: Well, I 3. missed my bus to work this morning. I hailed a taxi, but there was so much traffic! I arrived to work late.
Wei: Uh-oh. Did you call work?
Erica: I called, but nobody picked up the phone. I paid the taxi, but then I dropped my phone in the taxi.
Wei: Oh no! Did you lose your phone?
Erica: Thankfully, the taxi driver still has it. I asked him 4. to drop it off at the police station on Main Street.
Wei: Now I understand. I called you twice, but you didn't pick up. I was worried.
Erica: Sorry, Wei. I wanted to call you, but I didn't memorize your number.
Wei: So then what happened? Did your boss understand?
Erica: Actually, no. My job has a strict late policy. If you're late twice, you get automatically fired. So my boss fired me.
Wei: No way!
Erica: I'm glad I made it to your dinner. This just may be the best part of my day.
Wei: Yeah… about that. I burned the curry. It is very black.
Erica: Ha ha! 5. Just my luck!
Wei: Well, do you want to go out to eat?
Erica: Sure, that sounds great.

Substitution Drill: Use the following responses in the above conversation.

		A. FORMAL	B. INFORMAL
1.	What's wrong?	Is everything alright?	What's the matter?
2.	What happened?	Do you want to talk about it?	Tell me about it.
3.	missed my bus to work	was too late to catch the bus	was running too late for the bus
4.	to drop it off at	if he could leave it at the	to bring it to the
5.	Just my luck!	I guess my luck is not changing!	That is par for the course!

CULTURAL NOTE:

When Erica says she "hailed a taxi", the verb "to hail" in this instance means "to raise your hand" to signal an approaching taxi to stop. In Korean, "택시를 불러 세우다."

(Erica가 자기가"hailed a taxi" 했다고 말할 때 동사 "to hail"은 다가오는 택시를 세우기 위해 손을 들었다는 것을 의미합니다. 한국어로 표현하면 "택시를 불러세우다."라는 의미입니다.)

- To **get fired** means you were terminated from employment.
- "If you're late, you **get fired** automatically." (지각하면 무조건 해고를 당한다.)

When Wei tells Erica that he burned the curry, Erica exclaims, "Just my luck!" This is sarcasm. Erica is commenting on her luck because it seems only unlucky things are happening to her. People say this when bad or inconvenient things happen to them.

(Wei가 Erica에게 카레를 태웠다고 말할 때 Erica는 "Just my luck!"이라고 말합니다. 이것은 빈정대는 표현입니다. Erica는 불운한 일들만 자기에게 생기는 것 같기 때문에 자신의 운에 대해 말하는 것입니다. 사람들은 재수가 없거나 불편한 일이 자신에게 생길 때 이렇게 말을 합니다.)

Grammar Gallery 2: *Yes / No Questions in the Past*

Asking questions about the past and negative responses about the past.

YES / NO QUESTIONS

Did	I	watch	a movie	yesterday? last night? on the weekend? →	Yes,	I	did.
	you					you	
	we					we	
	they					they	
	he					he	
	she					she	
	it					it	
Did	I	watch	a movie	yesterday? last night? on the weekend? →	No,	I	did not. (didn't)
	you					you	
	we					we	
	they					they	
	he					he	
	she					she	
	it					it	

WWWWWH QUESTIONS

What	did	I / you / we / they / he / she / it	do	yesterday? / last night? / on the weekend?	➡	I / You / We / They / He / She / It	watched	a movie.
What	did	I / you / we / they / he / she / it	do	yesterday? / last night? / on the weekend?	➡	I / You / We / They / He / She / It	did not (didn't) watch	a movie.

Exercise 5 *Complete the questions.*

1. A: Did you go on a date last Friday? B: No, I didn't.
2. A: ____________ stay home yesterday? B: Yes, he did.
3. A: What ____________ watch last night? B: They watched movies.
4. A: What ____________ visit last weekend? B: She visited an art museum.
5. A: ____________ work last week? B: No, I didn't. I work this week.
6. A: Where ____________ work yesterday? B: They worked at the downtown office.
7. A: ____________ text her yet? B: Yes, he did. He texted her an hour ago.
8. A: Who ____________ talk to yesterday? B: I talked to my parents.
9. A: Why ____________ skip classes on Monday? B: She skipped because she had the flu.
10. A: When ____________ dance at Hongdae? B: We danced at Hongdae last Saturday.

Exercise 6 *Complete the answers. Use the schedule to answer the question in the past tense. If the answer is "No", then write what Gary actually did.*

Gary's Schedule for Last Week:

Monday	Tuesday	Wednesday	Thursday	Friday	Saturday	Sunday
Work at my part-time job	Study for English test	Watch a soccer match on T.V. with friends	Visit Jenny at the hospital	Try the new burger place	Clean the house Shop for clothes with mom	Start diet Jog around the neighborhood

1. A: Did Gary watch a movie last Monday?

   B: No, he didn't. He worked at his part-time job last Monday.
2. A: Did Gary study for his English test last Tuesday?

   B: ______________________________ .
3. A: Did Gary visit Jenny at the hospital last Wednesday?

   B: ______________________________ .
4. A: What did Gary do last Friday?

   B: ______________________________ .
5. A: What did Gary do last Saturday?

   B: ______________________________ .
6. A: Did Gary start a diet last Sunday?

   B: ______________________________ .

Exercise 7 *Mixed Exercise with Past Tense: Fill in the blanks with the correct form of the verb.*

1. What ________ he play yesterday? He ________ soccer.
2. When ________ she ________ her mother? She visited her mother last night.
3. ________ ________ study English last night? Yes, I ________ .
4. What mountain ________ he ________ last weekend? He hiked Mt. Surak.
5. ________ ________ dance last night? No, they ________ .
6. ________ ________ work hard yesterday? Yes, I ________ .

7. What time ________ I arrive this morning? You ________ at 8 a.m.

8. Why did we cry? We ________ because the movie was so sad.

9. How long ________ you ________ in Europe? I travelled for 2 months. It was great.

10. Who ________ she ________ in class? She texted her friend. She is a bad student.

Phrasal Verbs using "GO":

Exercise 8 *Write the correct phrasal verb next to the picture.*

go in	go out	go by	go on	go ahead
go through	go nuts	go across	go down	go up

The people ________ the entrance.
The people ________ the exit.

The hikers ________ the mountain.
The hikers ________ the mountain.

The cars ________ the tunnel.
The cars ________ the bridge.

The bicyclists ________ the old woman.

The children ________ in the playroom.
The woman lets the children ________ playing.

The bicyclist lets the woman ________ .

TOEIC VOCABULARY

Read the following common TOEIC words. Memorize so that you can do well on the TOEIC. Write the Korean and English in the space below two times to help you learn.

Predict: 예측하다.
Political magazines predicted that he would be re-elected.
정치관련 잡지들은 그가 재선될 것이라고 예측했다.

_____ / _____ _____ / _____

Preliminary: 예비의.
Sufficient discussions were preliminary to making a decision.
충분한 논의를 하는 것이 결정을 내릴 때 예비사항이다.

_____ / _____ _____ / _____

Presumably: 아마도.
Presumably, the football match has been cancelled for the threat of terror.
테러 위협 때문에 축구경기가 취소된 것 같다.

_____ / _____ _____ / _____

Previous: 이전의, 예전의.
Do you have any previous experience of this type of work?
이런 종류의 업무를 예전에 해 본 경험이 있습니까?

_____ / _____ _____ / _____

Primary: 우선적인, 일차적인.
Many of the residents rely on farming as their primary source of income.
많은 주민들이 주 수입원으로 농업에 의지한다.

_____ / _____ _____ / _____

Priority: 우선적으로 해야 할 일, 우선권, 선취권, 우위.
After several robberies in the area, security has become a high priority.
이 지역에서 몇 건의 강도사건이 발생한 뒤 치안이 가장 중요한 사안이 되었다.

_____ / _____ _____ / _____

Privatization: 사유화.
Water and power privatization is the core agenda of this meeting.
상수도와 전력 사유화가 이번 회합의 주요 의제이다.

_____ / _____ _____ / _____

Proceed: 나아가다.
Before proceeding further, we must define the terms and conditions of the contract.
더 진행하기 전에 이번 계약의 조건을 정해야 한다.

_____ / _____ _____ / _____

Productivity: 생산성.
Management should introduce a new way of raising productivity.
사측은 새로운 생산성 향상 방안을 도입해야 한다.

_____ / _____ _____ / _____

Professional: 전문적인, 직업적인.
What professional qualifications does the applicant have?
그 지원자가 어떤 전문적인 자격들을 지니고 있습니까?

_____ / _____ _____ / _____

Profit: 이익.
The company made a huge profit on the deal.
우리 회사는 이번 거래에서 상당한 이익을 창출했다.

_____ / _____ _____ / _____

Prohibit: 금지하다.
They are prohibited from revealing personal details about the candidates.
후보자들에 대한 개인적인 사항을 유출하는 것은 금지되어 있다.

_____ / _____ _____ / _____

Prolong: 연기하다.
I don't want to prolong the conversation with her.
그녀와의 대화를 질질 끌고 싶지 않다.

_____ / _____ _____ / _____

Prominent: 두드러진.
The monument is in a prominent position outside the police station.
그 기념물은 경찰서 밖의 눈에 잘 띄는 위치에 있다.

_____ / _____ _____ / _____

Promising: 전도가 유망한.
The lawyer will have a promising career in law

in the future.
그 변호사는 장차 법조계에서 유망한 경력을 쌓을 것이다.

_________ / _________ _________ / _________

Properly: 적당히.
Parents should teach their children to behave properly in public places.
부모들은 자녀들이 공공 장소에서 예의 바르게 행동하도록 가르쳐야 한다.

_________ / _________ _________ / _________

Property: 재산.
The hotel is not responsible for any damage to guests' personal property.
호텔 측은 투숙객의 개인 재산에 가해진 어떤 피해에도 책임이 없습니다.

_________ / _________ _________ / _________

Proportion: 비율.
The proportion of women graduates has increased in recent years.
여성 졸업자의 비율이 최근 증가하였습니다.

_________ / _________ _________ / _________

Prospective: 전망이 있는, 예상의.
The prospective costs of providing pensions for the elderly will be enormous.
노년층에게 연금을 제공하기 위한 예상 비용이 엄청날 것입니다.

_________ / _________ _________ / _________

Publicity: 공표, 선전, 홍보.
Standards in education have received much publicity over the last few years in Korea.
지난 몇 년에 걸쳐 한국에서는 교육의 표준이 많이 홍보가 되었다.

_________ / _________ _________ / _________

Radically: 근본적으로, 급진적으로.
A radically different method of production should be adopted to improve productivity.
생산성을 향상시키기 위해서는 근본적으로 다른 생산방식을 도입해야 한다.

_________ / _________ _________ / _________

Reduction: 감소.
The company promised they would make no staff reductions for at least two years.
최소 2년 간은 직원 감축이 없을 것이라고 회사는 약속하였다.

_________ / _________ _________ / _________

Refrain: 자제하다.
Please refrain from smoking in this area.
이 곳에서는 금연하시기 바랍니다.

_________ / _________ _________ / _________

Regarding: ~에 관하여.
Regarding your recent inquiry, I have enclosed a copy of our new brochure.
귀하의 최근 문의에 대해 새로 나온 안내책자 한 부를 동봉해 드렸습니다.

_________ / _________ _________ / _________

Regardless of: ~에 관계없이.
The law requires equal treatment for all, regardless of race, religion, or sex.
법은 인종, 종교 또는 성별에 관계없이 모든 이에게 동등한 대우를 요구한다.

_________ / _________ _________ / _________

Regional: 지역적인.
Local and regional governments try to make money on their own.
지방자치 정부들은 스스로 수익을 내려고 노력한다.

_________ / _________ _________ / _________

Regulation: 규정.
All companies must comply with the labor union regulations.
모든 기업은 노동조합 관련 규정을 준수해야 한다.

_________ / _________ _________ / _________

Reimbursement: 보상.
You can get the reimbursement for the expenses of your travel to England from the company.
당신은 회사로부터 영국 여행 비용에 대한 보상을 받을 수 있다.

_________ / _________ _________ / _________

Release: 해제, 방출, 공개, 석방, 해방.
Before release, the polar bears will be fitted with electronic tracking devices.
놓아주기 전에 북극 곰에게는 전자 추적장치가 부착될 것이다.

_________ / _________ _________ / _________

Remarkable: 주목할 만한, 상당한.
It is remarkable that women were not able to vote until that time.
그 때까지 여성들은 투표권이 없었다는 것은 주목할 만하다.

_________ / _________ _________ / _________

UNIT

4 The Movies Yesterday

Review Questions:

1. What do you dislike doing?

   I dislike ______________________________ .

   (activity verb +ing)

2. What do you enjoy doing?

   I enjoy ______________________________ .

   (activity verb +ing)

Warm-up Questions:

10. What kind of movies do you like to watch?

    I like to watch ____________________ .

    (genre)

11. What is your favorite movie? Who was in it?

    My favorite movie is ____________________ . ____________________ was in it.

    (movie title) (actor name)

12. What is your favorite movie theater treat?

    My favorite movie theater treat is ____________________ .

    (treat name)

Popular Actors:
Jennifer Lawrence
Scarlet Johansson
Julia Roberts
Angelina Jolie
Kristen Stewart
Robert Downey Jr.
Jackie Chan
Bradley Cooper
Vin Diesel
Tom Cruise

Popular movies:
Avatar
Titanic
Jurassic World
The Avengers
Harry Potter
Frozen
Iron Man
Lord of the Rings
Transformers
Toy Story

Popular snacks:
Chocolate bars
Jelly Beans
Skittles
Licorice
Popcorn
Nachos
Hot Dog
Potato Chips
Buttered Squid

Popular genres of movies:
Action
Animation
Biography
Comedy
Crime
Documentary
Drama
History
Horror

Dialogue A: *"Two Dates"*

Erica: How was your weekend?

Marco: Hi, Erica. It was epic! I went on two blind dates. One was in Hyehwa and the other was in at Samseong Station. I think I am in love.

Erica: Sounds like you had a better weekend than I did. I just stayed home with my dog and relaxed. I looked after my younger sister who had the flu. 1. So give me the scoop!

Marco: I went to Hyewha with my first date. We wanted to go see a musical, 2. but all the tickets were sold out. So we walked over to the CGV and ended up seeing "Iron Man". I actually like comedies more than action movies, but it was worth watching. I think Robert Downey Jr. is a great actor.

Erica: Did you see any of his movies when he was younger? 3. He is so good-looking. I remember seeing him in Chaplin. He was so convincing. Anyway, tell me more about your date.

Marco: It was good, but don't think we will meet up again. I think she just broke up with someone. I never asked, 4. but my gut feeling was that she was not ready for a serious relationship. However, I think we will remain friends.

Erica: That's great! So I assume that your second date was the best. What happened on Saturday?

Marco: Well, I met an old classmate of mine. 5. I have had a crush on her since elementary school. We went out for dinner and had some great food at a buffet. Then we went to Megabox and watched Toy Story. We shared some popcorn.

Erica: Sounds like love to me!

Substitution Drill: Use the following responses in the above conversation.

		A. FORMAL	B. INFORMAL
1.	So give me the scoop!	Please tell me the exciting story!	Tell me the news!
2.	but all the tickets were sold out.	but there were no more tickets available.	but they had sold all of the tickets by the time we got there.
3.	He is so good-looking.	He has always been such a handsome man.	He is always so attractive.
4.	but my gut feeling was	but I got the impression	I had an odd feeling
5.	I have had a crush on her	I have liked her a lot	I have been head over heels for her

Conversation Corner: *Simple Past Usage*

1.	**Finished events in the past with no connection to the present:** (현재와 아무 관계 없이 과거에 종료된 사건들) • King Sejong **invented** Hangul. • The Japanese **invaded** Korea.
2.	**With a finished time word:** (과거를 가리키는 단어와 함께) • I **went** to the park yesterday. • We **visited** Korea in 2003.
3.	**For stories / lists of events:** (과거에 발생한 사건들을 순서대로 열거) • He **went** to a café, **sat** down and **had** a tea. • Yesterday I **went** to the shopping mall, **met** a friend for dinner, and **played** computer games.
4.	**Details of news:** (구체적인 사실) • I've hurt my back. I **fell** off my bike. • I've been on holiday. I **went** to Jeju.
5.	**As part of the second conditional:** (가정법 과거: 현재 사실에 대한 반대 진술을 할 때) • If I **passed** the test, I would have less stress. • If she **won** the lottery, she would travel the world.

What did you do last week?

Where did you go on vacation?

Who did you meet?

When did you graduate?

When did you wake up?

Who did their homework?

What did you do yesterday?

What did you do on Chuseok?

Who ate breakfast?

Why did she miss the exam?

NOTE: The most common questions use **"do"**, which can be replaced by any other verb easily. (가장 보편적인 질문에서 "do"를 사용하는데 이것은 다른 동사로 쉽게 대체할 수 있습니다.)

- What did you **do** last weekend?
  I went to Sinsaegae and bought some clothing.
- What did you **do** last summer?
  I travelled around Bali and South Indonesia.

This question is usually the next question after "How are you?"

Work in a group and make six questions to ask other students or your professor. Use the form– "Where did...", "Who did...", "Why did..." and "When did...".

Grammar Gallery 1: *Simple Past Tense Irregular*

Look at the sentence below:

I ate pizza. I didn't eat pizza. Did you eat pizza?

This is an example of an **"irregular verb"** because it doesn't follow the "+ ed" rule.

eat ➡ eated ✘ eat ➡ ate ✔

Simple Past Tense with Irregular verbs: no "+ ed"

These verbs don't follow the normal rule, and you have to memorize them. The following is a list of some common irregular verbs but not all. The more you use them in sentences talking with others, the easier it will be to remember.
(이러한 동사들은 통상적인 규칙을 따르지 않기 때문에 암기를 해야 합니다. 다음 도표는 자주 사용되는 불규칙 동사 목록입니다. 타인과 대화할 때 이러한 동사를 자주 사용할수록 기억하기 쉽습니다.)

green = regular (ed) blue = irregular (no ed)

Pronoun	Affirmative	Negative(not)	Inquisitive?(Question)	
I	played	didn't play	Did I play... ?	Yes, I did. / No, I didn't.
You	went	didn't go	Did you go... ?	Yes, you did. / No, you didn't.
We	ate	didn't eat	Did we eat... ?	Yes, we did. / No, we didn't.
They	studied	didn't study	Did they study... ?	Yes, they did. / No, they didn't.
He	did	didn't do	Did he play... ?	Yes, he did. / No, he didn't.
She	worked	didn't work	Did she go... ?	Yes, she did. / No, she didn't.
It	drank	didn't drink	Did it eat... ?	Yes, it did. / No, it didn't.

Infinitive	Past Simple	Infinitive	Past Simple	Infinitive	Past Simple
be*	was / were	forget	forgot	**run***	ran
begin	began	**get***	got	**say***	said
break	broke	**give***	gave	**see***	saw
build	built	**go***	went	sell	sold
buy*	bought	grow	grew	send	sent
catch	caught	**have***	had	shut	shut
choose	chose	**hear***	heard	**sing***	sang
come*	came	hide	hid	**sit***	sat
cut	cut	hit	hit	**sleep***	slept
cost	cost	hold	held	**stand***	stood
dig	dug	hurt	hurt	steal	stole
do*	did	know	knew	**swim***	swam
draw	drew	**leave***	left	**take***	took
drink*	drank	lose	lost	**teach***	taught
eat*	ate	**make***	made	**think***	thought
fall	fell	**meet***	met	throw	threw
feel*	felt	pay	paid	understand	understood
fight	fought	put	put	**wear***	wore
find	found	**read***	read	win	won
fly	flew	ride	rode	**write***	wrote

(* Most common verbs)

MEMORY TIPS: Write the irregular past tense in the space provided.

Group 1: "– ught"

a. bring –
b. teach –
c. fight –
d. seek –
e. buy –
f. think –

Group 2: "ow" → "ew"

a. grow –
b. know –
c. throw –
d. blow –
e. fly* –
* (a bit different)

Group 3: small words that end in "t"

a. hit –
b. hurt –
c. cut –
d. cost –
e. put –
f. shut –
* "sit" "eat" "get" "meet"
– don't follow rule!

Group 4: "i" to "a"

drink –
sing –
begin –

Group 5: "end" to "ent"

send –
spend –
lend –
bend –

Exercise 1 *Practice with a partner. One person looks at the book and says the regular form (infinitive) and the partner says the past tense. Take turns asking and answering. Try to learn the lists above.*

A. drink

B. drank D-R-A-N-K

B. My turn: sing

A. sang S-A-N-G

Exercise 2 *Fill in the blanks with the correct past tense of the verb.*

1. I ______________ (bring) some pencils to class.
2. She ______________ (hear) a new song on the radio.
3. You ______________ (read) three books last week.
4. We ______________ (speak) French to the waitress.
5. They ______________ (understand) during the class, but now he doesn't understand.
6. I ______________ (forget) to buy some milk.
7. She ______________ (lose) her keys last week.
8. I ______________ (swim) last week.
9. They ______________ (know) the answer yesterday.
10. We ______________ (lend) some money to Billy.
11. The children ______________ (sleep) in the airplane.
12. I ______________ (choose) pizza for dinner.
13. The film ______________ (begin) right on time.
14. She ______________ (fly) to Vancouver.

Exercise 3 *Write the answers in the negative (didn't).*

1. I ______________(bring) a pencil to class.
2. She ______________(hear) a new song on the radio.
3. You ______________ (read) three books last week.
4. We ______________ (speak) French to the waitress.
5. They ______________ (understand) during the class.
6. I ______________(forget) to buy some milk.
7. She ______________ (lose) her keys last week.
8. I ______________(swim) last week.
9. They ______________ (know) the answer yesterday.

Exercise 4 *Make and answer the Past Tense Yes / No Questions below:*

1. ________ the children ________ (sleep) in the airplane? Yes, ________ ________ .
2. ________ you ________ (choose) pizza for dinner? No, ________ ________ .
3. ________ the film ________ (begin) right on time? Yes, ________ ________ .
4. ________ she ________ (fly) to Vancouver? Yes, ________ ________ .
5. ________ they ________ (drive) to Busan? No, ________ ________ .
6. ________ she ________ (teach) English at the university? Yes, ________ ________ .
7. ________ you ________ (send) me an e-mail earlier? No, ________ ________ .
8. ________ we ________ (leave) the house at 6:45 a.m.? No, ________ ________ .
9. ________ he ________ (feel) terrible after eating the rare meat? Yes, ________ ________ .

Exercise 5 *Survey Time: Ask 10 different people!*

NAME:	What did you do last weekend?

Dialogue B: *"I have some bad news."*

Marco: I just turned on my computer and got your message on Facebook. Why didn't you just text me on my phone? Your message was a bit vague. 1. Is something wrong?

Erica: I felt a little awkward. I have some good news and some bad news. Which would you like first?

Marco: Ouch! 2. That's never good to hear. Let's get it over with. What's the bad news?

Erica: I went shopping in Hongdae today. When I was in the store, I saw that girl you are dating. I remembered her because of the picture you showed me. She was with another guy. They held hands and I saw them kiss outside.

Marco: I guess 3. she never moved on like she said she did. I was a bit skeptical about us. She kept getting text messages from someone. One time she got a call and just hung up. Then she turned off her phone.

Erica: I hate to gossip, but felt you needed to know. I hope you cheer up soon.

Marco: Well, that certainly changes my day and plans. Oh well. These things happen. 4. There are plenty of fish in the sea. What's the good news?

Erica: Well, one of my dart league members moved last week and we need a fourth. I know you like darts and drinking, so I thought maybe you would like to join. It starts tonight.

Marco: Wow. That sounds great. I guess I'll be there around 7 at the usual place. Oh... I just thought of something. Isn't Elizabeth on the team?

Erica: I can see you are 5. already over the last girlfriend!

Substitution Drill: Use the following responses in the above conversation.

		A. FORMAL	B. INFORMAL
1.	Is something wrong?	Is there a problem?	Is everything OK?
2.	That's never good to hear.	I didn't want to hear that.	That's never good.
3.	she never moved on	she never got over the last boyfriend	she wasn't ready to be finished with her ex boyfriend
4.	There are plenty of fish in the sea.	There are other opportunities to be had.	There are other single ladies out there.
5.	already over the last girlfriend!	ready to start dating again.	bouncing back after the bad news.

Grammar Gallery 2: *Simple Past Tense WWWWWH*

Exercise 6 *Make your own questions with Past Tense IRREGULAR VERBS.*

- What did ____?
- Where did ____?
- Why did ____?
- When did ____?
- How did ____?

Exercise 7 *Use the verb in the question to fill in the blanks in the answer.*

1. When did you eat? We ______________ at 4:30 p.m.
2. What did she see? I think she ______________ her boyfriend.
3. When did they start work? They ______________ at 11:00 a.m.
4. Who did they respect? They ______________ their teacher.
5. What kind of coffee did you order? I ______________ a caramel macchiato.
6. Where did they meet? They ______________ at the zoo.

7. How much did she work? She __________ too much.

8. How long did the movie take? I thought it __________ too long.

9. What did you want to drink? I __________ to drink an Americano.

10. Why did you come late yesterday? I __________ late because I forgot to set my alarm last night.

Exercise 8 *Make Questions: Complete the sentences using the proper question and verb forms.*

1. What __________ you __________ last night? I ate pizza last night.
2. Where __________ he __________ his shoes? He bought his shoes at the Adidas store.
3. When __________ you __________ to bed? We went to bed at midnight.
4. Who __________ you __________ ? I called my parents.
5. __________ you __________ to the wedding? No, I didn't. I didn't go to the wedding.
6. What __________ you __________ ? I had to go to his birthday party.
7. __________ she __________ English yesterday? Yes, she did. She taught four English classes.
8. __________ you __________ me an e-mail earlier? No, I didn't send you an email.
9. When __________ we __________ the house? We left at 6:45 a.m. this morning.
10. What kind of coffee __________ you __________ ? I drank a caramel macchiato.

Exercise 9 *What do you remember? Fill in as many as you can with your partner! Don't look at the answers. Who has the most?*

Infinitive	Past Simple	Infinitive	Past Simple	Infinitive	Past Simple
be	______	forget	______	run	______
begin	______	get	______	say	______
break	______	give	______	see	______
build	______	go	______	sell	______
buy	______	grow	______	send	______
catch	______	have	______	shut	______
choose	______	hear	______	sing	______
come	______	hide	______	sit	______
cut	______	hit	______	sleep	______
cost	______	hold	______	stand	______
dig	______	hurt	______	steal	______
do	______	know	______	swim	______
draw	______	leave	______	take	______
drink	______	lose	______	teach	______
eat	______	make	______	think	______
fall	______	meet	______	throw	______
feel	______	pay	______	understand	______
fight	______	put	______	wear	______
find	______	read	______	win	______
fly	______	ride	______	write	______

Phrasal Verbs using "MAKE":

Phrasal Verb	Meaning	Example
make for	**a.** to go toward something (~을 향해 가다.) **b.** to add to (추가하다.)	**a.** Make for the classroom. We are running late. **b.** S'mores make for a great camping experience.
make __ into	**a.** change something (변화시키다.)	**a.** They made my bedroom into an exercise room.

make off with	**a.** to leave with something, possibly stealing it (훔쳐가다.)	**a.** The thieves made off with my T.V. and stereo.
make out	**a.** slang for kissing (속어로 키스하다.) **b.** result of something (결과를 내다.)	**a.** The couple didn't watch the movie. They were making out the whole time. **b.** How did you make out fishing? Terrible. There were no bites.
make up	**a.** to lie / create a false story (거짓말을 꾸며내다.) *(noun) powder / color to apply to face (얼굴을 꾸미다.)	**a.** The boy made up a story about a monster.
make up for	**a.** to do something to replace a loss (보상하다, 상쇄하다.)	**a.** He made up for being late by showing up early the next date.

Exercise 10 *Use the above phrasal verbs in the sentences below.*

1. A: Oh no! The teacher is doing a homework check. What should I say?
   B: Quickly. ________ something ________ ! Say your dog ate it!
2. The deer ________ ________ the forest when they saw the hunters.
3. To ________ ________ ________ not getting his girlfriend a White Day present, he took her to her favorite restaurant.
4. A: How was the movie?
   B: Terrible. I don't like romantic dramas. It is just a bunch of people who ________ and then it gets sad.
5. Let's get an ice cream cake too. It will ________ ________ a better birthday party.
6. A: We just got back from the casino.
   B: Did you do well?
   A: We ________ ________ really well. We have 100 dollars more now.
7. Don't ________ ________ ________ my textbook. I need it back after you are done with it.
8. I am going to ________ my vegetables ________ a nice salad.

TOEIC VOCABULARY

Read the following common TOEIC words. Memorize so that you can do well on the TOEIC. Write the Korean and English in the space below two times to help you learn.

Notify: 통지하다, 알리다.
In January, we were notified that our article had been rejected.
1월에 우리 논문이 거절되었다는 통지를 받았다.

_________ /_________ _________ /_________

Numerous: 수많은.
The two businessmen have worked together on numerous projects.
두 사업가는 많은 사업을 함께 해 왔다.

_________ /_________ _________ /_________

Obstacle: 장애물.
Fear of English is an obstacle to getting a decent job.
영어 울렁증은 좋은 직업을 구하는 데 장애물이다.

_________ /_________ _________ /_________

Obtain: 획득하다.
Further information can be obtained from any branch office.
주가 정보는 어느 지사에서라도 구할 수 있습니다.

_________ /_________ _________ /_________

Occur: 발생하다.
The highest rates of unemployment occur in the downtown areas.
최고 실업률은 도심지에서 발생한다.

_________ /_________ _________ /_________

On account of: ~때문에.
She was told not to carry heavy luggage, on account of her wrist problem.
그녀는 손목에 문제가 있어서 무거운 짐을 들지 말라고 들었다.

_________ /_________ _________ /_________

On behalf of: ~를 위하여, ~대신에
On behalf of my alma mater, I wish to express gratitude.
모교를 대신하여 감사를 표하고 싶습니다.
She asked her lover to speak to her parents on her behalf.
그녀는 애인에게 자기 대신 자기 부모님께 말해달라고 요청했다.

_________ /_________ _________ /_________

On the wane: 쇠락해 가는.
By the 5th century, the power of the Roman Empire was on the wane.
5세기경 로마 제국의 세력은 기울어졌다.

_________ /_________ _________ /_________

Optimistic: 낙천적인.
Korean nationals are optimistic about the future of their motherland.
한국인들은 모국의 미래에 대해 낙관하고 있다.

_________ /_________ _________ /_________

Outcome: 결과.
The plaintiff was surprised at the outcome of the trial.
원고는 재판 결과에 대해 놀랐다.

_________ /_________ _________ /_________

Outdated: 한물간, 구식의.
This speculation is not credible due to the outdated figures used for it.
이번 예상에 사용된 수치가 오래되었기 때문에 신뢰할 수 없다.

_________ /_________ _________ /_________

Outline: 대강.
A debt reduction scheme of several shipbuilding companies was approved in outline.
조선업체 몇 곳의 부채삭감 계획이 대략적으로 승인되었다.

_________ /_________ _________ /_________

Output: 배출, 산출.
The output of carbon dioxide all over the world is enormous.
전 세계의 이산화탄소 배출량이 어마어마하다.

_________ /_________ _________ /_________

Overall: 전반적인.
The overall result of contraception is a decrease in population.

피임의 전반적인 결과는 인구 감소이다.

_______ / _______ _______ / _______

Overbook: 초과 예약하다.
This flight was heavily overbooked.
이번 비행편은 지나치게 초과 예약되었다.

_______ / _______ _______ / _______

Overdue: 마감일이 경과한.
People welcome this announcement but think it's long overdue.
사람들은 이번 발표를 환영하지만 너무 늦었다고 생각한다.

_______ / _______ _______ / _______

Overhead: 기본비용.
Their head office is in London so the overheads are very high.
그들의 본사가 런던에 있기 때문에 기본 비용이 매우 높다.

_______ / _______ _______ / _______

Overview: 개관, 조망.
This document includes a general overview of the admission regulations.
이 문서는 입학 규정에 대한 전반적인 개관을 담고 있다.

_______ / _______ _______ / _______

Overwork: 과로하다.
You deserve taking a week off because you have been overworking.
당신은 과로를 해 왔으니 1주일 휴가를 받을 자격이 있다.

_______ / _______ _______ / _______

Patronize: 후원하다, 애용하다.
I appreciate your patronizing my restaurant.
저희 식당을 애용해 주셔서 감사합니다.

_______ / _______ _______ / _______

Pending: ~까지.
Sales of this medicine have been stopped, pending further announcement.
이 약품의 판매는 다음 발표가 있을 때까지 중지되었다.

_______ / _______ _______ / _______

Perceive: 인식하다.
Young as she was, she had been perceived as a future chief executive.
어렸지만 그녀는 미래의 사장으로 인식되어 왔다.

_______ / _______ _______ / _______

Periodically: 주기적으로.
Teachers should meet periodically to discuss progress.
선생님들은 주기적으로 만나 진도를 상의한다.

_______ / _______ _______ / _______

Permanent: 영원한.
Nothing is permanent on earth.
지구상에 영원한 것은 아무 것도 없다.

_______ / _______ _______ / _______

Permission: 승인, 허락.
He obtained permission from his boss to go on a sick leave.
그는 사장님으로부터 병가를 가도 좋다는 승인을 받았다.

_______ / _______ _______ / _______

Persuasive: 설득력이 있는.
The opposition party has given a very persuasive argument against capital punishment.
야당은 사형 제도에 반대하는 매우 설득력이 있는 주장을 전개했다.

_______ / _______ _______ / _______

Pollute: 오염시키다.
Particles emitted from cars pollute the air more than yellow dusts flowing from China.
승용차가 배출하는 분진이 중국에서 불어오는 황사보다 공기를 더 오염시킨다.

_______ / _______ _______ / _______

Positive: 긍정적인.
The fact that he's breathing on his own again is a positive sign of recovery.
그가 다시 자가호흡을 한다는 사실은 긍정적인 회복의 조짐이다.

_______ / _______ _______ / _______

Possess: 소유하다.
He was found guilty of possessing prohibited items such as bullets and knives.
그는 총알과 도검 같은 금지품목을 소지하여 유죄 판명되었다.

_______ / _______ _______ / _______

Precisely: 정확하게.
It is difficult to predict precisely how much influence the changes will bring.
그런 변화가 정확하게 얼마나 많은 영향을 가져올지 예측하기는 어렵다.

_______ / _______ _______ / _______

UNIT 5 Let's Go Bowling!

Review Questions:

1. What kind of movies do you like to watch?

   I like to watch ______________________________ .
   (movie genre)

2. What is the best thing you did during your vacation?

   During my vacation, I ______________________________ .
   (fun activity)

What do the pictures below show?

Warm-up Questions:

Use the picture on the previous page to help you make your own answer.

13. What is the best place to meet friends / a colleague / a date? Why?

Ex. The best place to meet my friends is a coffee shop because we can drink coffee and chat easily.

- The best place to meet friends is ________________ (place) because ________________ (reason why).
- The best place to meet a colleague is ________________ (place) because ________________ (reason why).
- The best place to meet a date is ________________ (place) because ________________ (reason why).

14. If you could go anywhere right now, where would you go? Why?

I would go to ________________ (place / city / country name) because ________________________________ (reason why).

15. What would you do if you were meeting your friends but they were late?

If my friends were late, I would ________________________________ (activity).

Conversation Corner: *Arranging a meeting*

arrive	early	late	on time	punctual
organized	schedule	meeting	traffic	forget

Dear Diary… October 2nd

Today was a good day. I organized a meeting with some old friends. This was difficult because our schedules are so different. I arrived early, but Michelle and Tiffiny were late. Michelle was stuck in traffic, but Tiffiny just forgot about it. She is never punctual. Maybe one day she will be on time for something! Despite this, we still had fun!

Exercise 1 *Match the words from the previous page with their definitions.*

______ (noun)	When people come together for a specific purpose.	______ (adj.)	after the correct time
______ (adj.)	Doing something before the agreed time.	______ (adj.)	being on time, not late
______ (noun)	a build-up of vehicles which can slow down movement.	______ (verb)	not remember something.
______ (verb)	to have arranged a meeting	______ (noun)	a list of arrangements
______ (phrase)	arriving or departing at the correct time	______ (adj.)	arriving exactly on time as a habit, routine

Exercise 2 *Use the words above to complete the second diary entry.*

Dear Diary… October 2nd

I had a ______ with my manager yesterday. I arrived ______ because the ______ on the roads was terrible. When I arrived, she asked if I often ______ meetings and times. I told her I remembered the meeting, but couldn't be ______ only this once. She was angry and told me to be more ______ in the future. "I will ______ 30 minutes ______ next time!" I said. She told me to check my ______ for my free days and we ______ another meeting for next week. I was lucky.

Dialogue A: *"Late again?"*

Michelle: So, Tiffiny… 1. what was the last movie you watched?

Tiffiny: I saw Deadpool just last week. It was really good. It was a bit violent but the dialogue was funny,

Michelle: Oh! 2. You liked that? I thought it was kind of boring.

Tiffiny: 3. I'm not surprised. We always disagree about films.

Michelle: Right! Ha ha!

Tiffiny: What about yourself? What was your last film?

Michelle: It has been so long that I can hardly remember. I think it was Avengers 2.

Tiffiny: Wow! 4. That was ages ago! You have to get out more often. Hey, where is Marco? He should be here by now.

Michelle: He's always late! We should have arranged to meet earlier. Oh look! He's calling you.

Tiffiny: [answers phone] Marco! Where are you?

Marco: I'm sorry. I missed the bus. I'm going there now.

Tiffiny: Well, hurry up! The film starts in three minutes.

Marco: I'm pretty close, but not sure if I'm going to make it on time. The traffic is terrible. Sorry! 5. I'll be there as soon as I can. Bye! [Marco hangs up]

Tiffiny: Just hurry… he hung up!

Michelle: That guy! Let's just go in and find our seats.

Tiffiny: Shouldn't we wait for him?

Substitution Drill: Use the following responses in the above conversation.

		A. FORMAL	B. INFORMAL
1.	what was the last movie you watched?	what did you see last time you went to a theatre?	what was the last flick you remember seeing?
2.	You liked that?	Did you think that was good?	You found that interesting?
3.	I'm not surprised.	I don't find that surprising.	Seems about right.
4.	That was ages ago!	That was longer ago than I expected.	That was a really long time ago!
5.	I'll be there as soon as I can.	I'll do my best to get there quickly.	I'll try to get there as fast as I can.

GROUP DISCUSSION:

If you were in this situation, would you be angry at Marco? Would you wait for him? Decide YES or NO, then give reasons for your answer.

Grammar Gallery 1: *Present Simple vs. Past Simple vs. Present Continuous*

PAST SIMPLE			PRESENT SIMPLE			PRESENT CONTINUOUS		
I	met	Sam yesterday.	I	meet	Sam everyday.	I	am meeting	Sam today.
You			You			You	are meeting	
We			We			We		
They			They			They		
He			He	meets		He	is meeting	
She			She			She		

Yes / No Questions

Did you **meet** Sam yesterday? (Use this structure for every question in the past simple, regardless of which pronoun is used.)	**Do** I **meet** Sam every day? **Do** you **meet** Sam every day? **Do** we **meet** Sam every day? **Do** they **meet** Sam every day? **Does** he **meet** Sam every day? **Does** she **meet** Sam every day?	**Am** I **meeting** Sam today? **Are** you **meeting** Sam today? **Are** we **meeting** Sam today? **Are** they **meeting** Sam today? **Is** he **meeting** Sam today? **Is** she **meeting** Sam today

CLUE WORDS: To determine which tense we need, we have clue words. In the table above, the clue words are:

- YESTERDAY ➡ simple past
- EVERY DAY ➡ simple present
- NOW ➡ present continuous

Exercise 3 *We are not limited to these three words though. Look at the words in the box and write them in the correct column according to tense.*

yesterday / every day / now / usually / always / right now /
at the moment / last week / two days ago

PAST SIMPLE	PRESENT SIMPLE	PRESENT CONTINUOUS
1.	4.	7.
2.	5.	8.
3.	6.	9.

Exercise 4 *Choose a verb from the box and complete the sentences. First, circle the time words. Then change the tense where necessary.*

watch / drink / meet / drive / walk / go / eat / take / listen / study

1. I watched a great movie yesterday.
2. Did you ______________ your car to work last week?
3. She always ______________ kimchi and rice.
4. Does he ______________ to music every day?
5. We are ______________ in the library at the moment.
6. Are they ______________ home now?
7. I usually ______________ friends on Friday.
8. Do you ______________ English conversation classes?
9. She ______________ along the river path two days ago.
10. We are ______________ coffee together right now.
11. I ______________ for the test all last week.
12. James never ______________ cola.
13. Hey! What are you ______________ ? Is that a taco salad?
14. I can't talk right now. I'm ______________ the car.
15. When does he ______________ to work?
16. Sarah ______________ dramas every Sunday.
17. I ______________ your ex-girlfriend last night. She acted pretty cold to me.
18. They are ______________ home at the moment.
19. Quiet! I'm ______________ to the professor right now.
20. Last night, I ______________ a long break.

Exercise 5 *Write the sentences from 1-10 again below. Change the tense to the new one required. Don't forget to change the time words as well.*

1. (present continuous) I am watching a great movie now.
2. (present continuous) ______________________
3. (present continuous) ______________________
4. (simple present) ______________________
5. (simple past) ______________________
6. (simple past) ______________________
7. (simple past) ______________________
8. (present continuous) ______________________
9. (simple present) ______________________
10. (simple present) ______________________

Asking "Wh~" questions is a great way to gain information.
The table below shows a few examples of these questions in each of the three tenses discussed in this unit.

Wh~ QUESTIONS		
PAST SIMPLE	**PRESENT SIMPLE**	**PRESENT CONTINUOUS**
Name: ______ • Who did you meet yesterday? • What did you do? • Why did you meet? • Where did you meet? • When did you go home?	Name: ______ • Who do you see every day? • What do you do together? • Why do you do that? • Where do you do that? • When do you do that?	Name: ______ • Who are you meeting today? • What are you going to do? • Why are you meeting them? • Where are you meeting them? • When are you meeting them?

Dialogue B: *"What Next...?"*

Michelle: That was a good film!

Tiffiny: Yeah, I enjoyed it, too. 1. What did you think, Marco?

Marco: It was okay. I didn't really understand it though.

Michelle: That's because you arrived late, Marco!

Tiffiny: Yeah. You should be more punctual.

Marco: Ha ha! Okay. It's still early. 2. Let's get some dinner.

Michelle: I don't want to eat now. I'm so full from all that popcorn.

Tiffiny: Me too. What shall we do?

Michelle: We could go bowling, or we could go to a singing room. That's always fun!

Marco: Oh no! I heard you sing before. You should not be allowed in a singing room!

Tiffiny: Ha ha! That's what makes it fun! 3. But I don't fancy a singing room tonight.

Marco: Right. Let's go bowling then. We should call P.K. He likes bowling.

Michelle: 4. Isn't he working tonight?

Marco: Yeah, but he should be finished soon.

Michelle: Cool. Maybe he can teach you how to bowl then, Marco.

Tiffiny: Ha ha! I'll call him, but I don't think even P.K. can help Marco throw straight.

Marco: 5. Oh very funny, girls.

Substitution Drill: Use the following responses in the above conversation.

		A. FORMAL	B. INFORMAL
1.	What did you think,	What was your impression,	Did you enjoy it,
2.	Let's get some dinner.	Why don't we eat something?	Let's grab a bite to eat.
3.	But I don't fancy a	I'd rather not go to a	I'm not in the mood for a
4.	Isn't he working tonight?	I thought he was working.	Didn't he say he had to work?
5.	*Oh very funny,	*You are hilarious,	*Wow. That was so witty,

CULTURAL NOTE:

"Oh, very funny"(정말 재미있다), "You are hilarious"(너 참 재미있구나), and "Wow.That was so witty" (야 그거 참 재치 있네)와 같은 표현은 반어적으로 사용되고 있으며 정반대의 의미를 나타낸다.

Grammar Gallery 2: *The Imperative with LET'S*

To make a suggestion to someone, you can use "Let's". It is the contracted form of "Let us".

When you use "Let's", you must add a verb that expresses your suggestion. This form of the verb must be the infinitive form, no matter how many people you address. Look at the sentences below and practice saying them out loud. Then write two more examples of your own.

("Let' s"를 사용할 때에는 당신이 제안하는 내용을 표현하는 동사를 첨가해야 합니다. 이 때 동사의 형태는 당신이 몇 명의 사람들에게 말하는가에 관계 없이 원형이어야 합니다. 다음 문장을 보고 큰 소리로 연습해 보세요. 그리고 두 개의 예문을 스스로 써 보세요.)

Let's **play** football!	Let's **go** outside!	**Remember!!** "Let's" requires the infinitive form of the following verb, NOT the -ing form!
Let's **listen** to music!	Let's **watch** a movie!	
Let's **take** a walk!	Let's **get** something to drink!	
Let's ______________	Let's ______________	

Exercise 6 *Read the following statements. Then fill in the gaps with the suggestion. Use "Let's"!*

For example: Pedro wants to go to the cinema.
He says to Anna: "Let's go to the cinema."

1. Maria wants to prepare dinner.
   She says to Andreas: ______________________________
2. Andreas wants to have a party.
   He says to Maria: ______________________________
3. Julia wants to play tennis.
   She says to her friend: ______________________________
4. Anna wants to go inside.
   She says to her brother: ______________________________
5. Maria wants to invite the Smiths.
   She says to Andreas: ______________________________
6. Peter wants to watch a movie.
   He says to his brother: ______________________________

NOTE: We can also use "Let's" with a negative to express an undesirable course of action. This is achieved by simply adding the word NOT after "Let's". Here are some examples.

Affirmative sentences	Negative sentences
Let's ask the teacher.	Let's not ask the teacher.
Let's finish class early today.	Let's not finish class early today!

How should you study for a test? Make a few "Let's not..." suggestions and write them below.

Exercise 7 *Practice using "Let's" and "Let's not" with the following pictures:*

Example: A: I'm hot. Let's open the window.

B: No, let's not open the window. I'm cold!

1. open the window

2. order some food

3. climb Dobongsan

4. study together

5. get a drink

6. go to a singing room

Modal verbs: ***COULD*** *vs.* ***SHOULD***

The table shows how a basic sentence is constructed. As you can see, the structure is the same regardless of which modal verb is used.

pronoun	modal	verb	noun
We	could	drink	cola.
We	should	drink	cola.

So the structure is the same, but if you change the modal verb, the meaning is very different. Discuss in your group how they are different, and make notes in the box below.

Could or Should?

These two modal verbs have many functions in English, so it can be quite confusing knowing when to use them. Read the following explanations with a partner and discuss how these two words are different.

COULD	SHOULD
"Could" expresses an idea or an option revealing a strong opinion on the matter. "Could" is often used for offering ideas as possible solutions. ("Could"은 상황에 대한 강한 의견을 나타내는 생각이나 선택사항을 표현합니다. 또한 "Could"은 가능한 해결책으로서의 생각을 제안하기 위해서도 사용됩니다.)	"Should" expresses an opinion on which action to take: advice, a strong suggestion. It is more commonly used for peer advice, or between family members. ("Should"은 어떤 행동을 해야 할지에 관한 의견을 표현합니다: 즉 충고나 강한 제안 같은 것입니다. 동료나 가족 사이에서 충고를 할 때 더 일상적으로 사용됩니다.)
Example We **could** go bowling, or we could go to a singing room.	*Example* We **should** call PK. He likes bowling.

Exercise 8 *Decide whether each statement needs could or should. Or both!*

PROBLEM: My electricity bill was too high. How can I save money?

1. You ________ buy low-energy light bulbs. could / should
2. You ________ close all the doors and heat just one room. could / should
3. You ________ turn the thermostat lower. could / should
4. You ________ make sure all your doors and windows are seald tightly. could / should
5. You ________ turn off lights when you leave rooms. could / should
6. You ________ look into alternative energy sources for your home. could / should

Group Activity: Your group has been stranded on a desert island. Independently, think of 5 things each that your group should do in order to survive. Then discuss these ideas in your group. (여러분 조가 외딴 섬에 좌초하였습니다. 여러분 조가 생존하기 위해 해야 할 일을 각각 5가지씩 생각해 보세요. 그리고 조별로 그 생각을 토론해 보세요.)

7. We could ____.
8. We could ____.
9. We should ____.
10. We should ____.
11. We should ____.

EXPLORING IDIOMS

An idiom is a commonly used expression whose meaning does not relate to the literal meaning of its words. Below are a few idioms that contain the modal verbs "COULD" and "SHOULD", which we learned in this unit. Work in your group and try to match the idioms with their meanings. (숙어란 구성 단어들의 의미와 관계없는 의미를 지닌 일상적으로 사용되는 표현입니다. 다음의 숙어에는 이번 과에서 배운 조동사 "Could"과 "Should"이 포함되어 있습니다. 조별로 숙어와 그 의미를 연결해 보세요.)

Idioms	Meaning	Example
I could eat a horse.	a. I am very hungry. (I don't actually want to eat a horse, though.) (매우 배가 고프다. (하지만 정말로 말을 잡아 먹으려는 것은 아닙니다.))	a. I'm so ready to eat. I could eat a horse!
You could have fooled me.	a. something you say when you think the opposite may be true. (의도하지 않은 결과를 가져올 때 사용하는 표현.)	a. A: Really! I'm not angry! B: You could have fooled me! You sound very angry.

You could cut the tension with a knife.	a. said when a situation is very serious, and something potentially bad may happen. The reference to "knife" means the tension is so thick, it is solid enough to be cut. (상황이 심각하여 나쁜 일이 발생할 수도 있는 상황에서 사용되는 표현. "칼"을 언급한 것은 자를 수 있을 정도로 긴장이 매우 크다는 의미.)	a. I saw Marco and his girlfriend fighting at the party. You could have cut the tension with a knife.
I could hear a pin drop.	a. to be very quiet, so quiet that even the smallest sound can be heard. (매우 조용하여 아주 작은 소리도 들릴 수 있는 상황.)	a. My building lost power last night. It was so quiet, you could hear a pin drop.
How should I know?	a. said when you don't have the answer, and don't understand why you could have the answer. (답을 모르는 상태인데 알고 있을 것이라고 생각하는 것을 이해할 수 없을 때 사용함.)	a. A: Hey Bob. What was the answer to the last question on the test? B: How should I know? I'm not in that class.
It's time we should be going.	a. said when you want to let the host know that it is time that you would like to leave. (당신이 떠나야 할 때라고 초대한 사람에게 말해야 할 때 사용함.)	a. Thank you for the meal and drinks, but I think it's time we should be going.
You should be so lucky!	a. said when you don't think something will really happen, but you wish it would. (무엇인가 발생하기를 원하지만 발생하지 않을 것이라고 생각할 때 사용하는 표현.)	a. A: I need to get a raise at my job. B: You should be so lucky. The bosses are not giving anyone raises.
I zigged when I should have zagged.	a. said when a person went the wrong direction, usually meaning a decision more than an actual movement. (실제 움직임을 가리키는 표현이라기보다는 결정에 대해 가리키는 표현으로서 잘못된 방향으로 가고 있다는 의미.)	a. The date was going so well. I should have brought her home. But instead, I asked her to a singing room. I zigged when I should have zagged.

Exercise 9 *Discuss the above idioms with a partner. Choose 3 and make a new sentence using the idioms correctly.*

1. ______________________________.
2. ______________________________.
3. ______________________________.

TOEIC VOCABULARY

Read the following common TOEIC words. Memorize so that you can do well on the TOEIC. Write the Korean and English in the space below two times to help you learn.

Instantly: 곧.
The new information on the admission was instantly available.
새로운 입시 정보는 즉시 입수할 수 있었다.

_________ / _________ _________ / _________

Instrument: 도구.
Funding start-up companies is an important instrument of economic development.
신생기업에 자금을 제공하는 것이 경제 발전의 중요한 도구이다.

_________ / _________ _________ / _________

Intelligent: 지적인.
Will there be intelligent beings on other planets like Mars?
화성과 같은 다른 행성에 지적인 생명체가 있을까?

_________ / _________ _________ / _________

Intention: 의도.
He thinks his boss has an intention of laying several staff off without prior notice.
그는 사장님이 사전 통지 없이 직원 몇 명을 해고하려는 의도를 지니고 있다고 생각한다.

_________ / _________ _________ / _________

Investigate: 조사하다.
The prosecutor is investigating the murder case with a prejudice.
검사는 편견을 가지고 살인 사건을 수사하고 있다.

_________ / _________ _________ / _________

Itinerary: 여행일정.
His itinerary would take him from Seoul to Busan.
그의 여행일정에 따르면 서울에서 부산으로 갈 것이다.

_________ / _________ _________ / _________

Journalist: 기자, 언론인.
Amanpour is the most famous journalist around the world.
Amanpour는 전 세계에서 가장 유명한 언론인이다.

_________ / _________ _________ / _________

Justify: 정당화하다.
Nothing justifies murdering another human being.
살인은 그 어느 것으로도 정당화할 수 없다.

_________ / _________ _________ / _________

Launch: 시작하다.
The Korean police plan to launch an investigation into the deal.
한국 경찰이 그 거래에 관한 조사를 시작할 계획이다.

_________ / _________ _________ / _________

Lease: 임대.
The landlord refused to renew his lease.
집주인은 임대를 갱신하기를 거부했다.

_________ / _________ _________ / _________

Lenient: 관대한.
Universities in Korea are too lenient to cheating in exams.
한국의 대학들은 시험의 부정행위에 대해 지나치게 관대하다.

_________ / _________ _________ / _________

Liable: 책임져야 할, ~하기 쉬운, ~할 것 같은.
People who are liable for income tax at a higher rate try to avoid being levied.
높은 세율의 소득세를 납부해야 하는 사람들은 과세를 피하려고 한다.

_________ / _________ _________ / _________

Likely: 그럴듯한.
I'd very likely have done the same thing in your situation.
네 입장이었다면 나도 마찬가지로 똑같이 처신했을 것이야.

_________ / _________ _________ / _________

Liquid: 액체의, 처분할 수 있는.
Children take antibiotics in liquid form.
어린이들은 액상 항생제를 먹는다.
Their shares are more liquid than those of other companies.
그들의 주식은 다른 회사의 주식보다 더 환금성이 높다.

_________ / _________ _________ / _________

Locate: 찾다.
Large shopping centers are located at the areas of high population density.
대형 상가는 높은 인구 밀집지역에 있다.

_________ / _________ _________ / _________

Lower: 낮추다.
Some stores have lowered the prices of the products they sell to attract more consumers.
일부 상점은 손님을 불러모으기 위해 판매제품의 가격을 인하했다.

_________ / _________ _________ / _________

Lucrative: 돈벌이가 되는.
He has inherited a lucrative business from his grandfather.
그는 할아버지로부터 수익이 나는 사업체를 물려받았다.

_________ / _________ _________ / _________

Malfunction: 오작동.
A malfunction in one of the engines has prevented the plane from taking off.
엔진 한 곳의 오작동으로 말미암아 비행기가 이륙을 하지 못했다.

_________ / _________ _________ / _________

Materialize: 구체화되다.
Problems were expected, but they never materialized.
문제가 예측되었지만 불거지지는 않았다.

_________ / _________ _________ / _________

Maximize: 최대로 하다.
The main purpose of almost all companies is to maximize profit.
거의 모든 회사의 주요 목적은 이익을 극대화하는 것이다.

_________ / _________ _________ / _________

Merger: 합병.
There are a lot of rumors about a merger with another leading bank.
다른 선도은행과의 합병에 관한 많은 소문이 있다.

_________ / _________ _________ / _________

Moderate: 중간의, 완화된.
Even a moderate amount of alcohol can be dangerous.
약간의 알코올 섭취만으로도 위험할 수 있다.

_________ / _________ _________ / _________

Morale: 사기.
The announcement of pay cuts will lower the morale of the staff.
급여 삭감 발표가 직원들의 사기를 낮출 것이다.

_________ / _________ _________ / _________

Motivate: 동기를 부여하다.
The profit-sharing plan is designed to motivate the staff to work hard.
직원들이 열심히 일하도록 동기를 부여하기 위해 이익 분배 계획이 정해진다.

_________ / _________ _________ / _________

Mutual: 상호의.
Mutual respect and fair profit-sharing are necessary for any partnership to work properly.
어떤 동업이라도 성공하기 위해서는 상호 존중과 공정한 이익 분배가 필요하다.

_________ / _________ _________ / _________

Necessarily: 반드시, 꼭.
Suffering from cancer does not necessarily mean death.
암을 앓고 있다고 해서 꼭 죽으란 법은 없다.

_________ / _________ _________ / _________

Necessity: 생필품.
In a refugee camp, people live without the basic necessities of life.
난민촌에서 사람들은 기본적인 생활 필수품도 없이 살아간다.

_________ / _________ _________ / _________

Negligence: 나태함, 게으름.
Residents sued the authorities concerned for their negligence in maintaining the reservoir.
주민들인 저수지 관리를 태만하게 한 관계당국자들을 고소했다.

_________ / _________ _________ / _________

Negotiate: 협상하다.
The French government always refuses to negotiate with terrorists.
프랑스 정부는 항상 테러리스트와의 타협을 거부한다.

_________ / _________ _________ / _________

Nominate: 지명하다.
Hillary will be the first woman to be nominated for the job of president.
Hillary는 대통령직에 지명된 최초의 여성이 될 것이다.

_________ / _________ _________ / _________

UNIT 1-5 REVIEW

Warm-up Questions:

1. How are you doing today? I'm doing ________________ .
2. How was your vacation? It was ________________ .
3. What was the best thing you did during the vacation?
   The best thing I did was ________________ .
4. When is your birthday? My birthday is ________________ .
5. Where did you have your birthday party?
   I had my birthday party at ________________ .
6. What presents did you get from your friends and family?
   I got ____________ , ____________ and ____________ .
7. What do you do in your free time? I ________________ .
8. What do you enjoy doing? I enjoy ________________ .
9. What do you dislike doing? I dislike ________________ .
10. What kind of movies do you like to watch?
    I like to watch ________________ .
11. What is your favorite movie and why?
    My favorite movie is __________ because ____________ .
12. What is your favorite movie theater treat? Why?
    My favorite __________ because ________________ .
13. What is the most beautiful place you know?
    The most beautiful place I know is ________________ .
14. Where would you go if you could go anywhere?
    If I could go anywhere, I would go to ________________ .
15. What do you do if your friends are late to the coffee shop?
    If my friends were late, I would ________________ .

Exercise 1 *Using words from the word bank below, complete the following 'simple present' sentences.*

like(s)	hate(s)	exercise(s)	work(s)	wake(s)
read(s)	run(s)	watch(es)	study / studies	drink(s)

1. I love to ____run____ by the lake in the morning.
2. He always ________ a lot on the weekend.
3. My father ________ in an office downtown.
4. I usually ________ up at 11 a.m. on Sunday.
5. People who ________ are usually quite healthy.
6. I ________ best when I am in the library.
7. My mom ________ American dramas on T.V.
8. They ________ getting up early in the morning.
9. I ________ to go on vacation.
10. I always ________ before I go to bed.

Exercise 2 *Unscramble the phrases below to make questions and statements in the 'present continuous' tense. You have to add the "be" verb and "ing". They are not supplied in the question.*

(아래의 구를 제대로 정렬하여 현재 진행형의 의문문이나 평서문으로 만들어 보세요. "be" 동사와 "ing" 형태를 첨가해야 합니다. 그것은 질문에 나와있지 않습니다.)

Ex. wear / today / ? / you / what ➡ What (are) you wear(ing) today?

1. run late / I / . / for class / right now

____

2. He / go / not / this weekend / . / soccer game / to the

____

3. live / these days / you / Where / ?

____

4. dance / under the stars / right now / . / They

____

5. When / they / lunch / eat / ? / today

6. the professor / now / about / talk / ? / What

7. not / exercise / now / He / . / at the gym

The "be" verb past tense:
The verb "be" has two forms in the past tense: WAS and WERE.

PRESENT TENSE

	Normal	Negative(not)	Question?	
I	am	am not	Am I...?	Yes, you are. No, you aren't.
You We They	are	are not (aren't)	Are they...?	Yes, they are. No, they aren't.
He She It	is	is not (isn't)	Is she...?	Yes, she is. No, she isn't.

PAST TENSE

	Normal	Negative(not)	Question?	
I	was	was not	Was I...?	Yes, you were. No, you weren't.
You We They	were	were not (weren't)	Were they...?	Yes, they were. No, they weren't.
He She It	was	was not (wasn't)	Was she...?	Yes, she was. No, she wasn't.

Exercise 3 *Using the chart above, choose the correct form of the "Past Simple" of the "be" verb: "was" or "were".*

1.	You ________ late for the bus yesterday. You ________ (not) late for the bus yesterday. ________ you late for the bus yesterday? Yes, I ________ / No, I ________ .
2.	They ________ all very fast runners. They ________ (not) all very fast runners. ________ they all very fast runners? Yes, they ________ . / No, they ________ .
3.	It ________ great to see them again. It ________ (not) great to see them again. ________ it great to see them again? Yes, it ________ . / No, it ________ .
4.	We ________ happy to finish school. We ________ (not) happy to finish school. ________ we happy to finish school? Yes, we ________ . / No, we ________ .
5.	He ________ a happy child. He ________ (not) a happy child. ________ he a happy child? Yes, he ________ . / No, he ________ .
6.	He ________ excited to see his sister again. He ________ (not) excited to see his sister again. ________ he excited to see his sister again? Yes, he ________ . / No, he ________ .

Exercise 4 *The "be" verb extra time! Complete the following dialogue between two friends. Use "wasn't" or "weren't".*

Tiffiny: Hi Michelle. How are you?

Michelle: I'm good, thanks. Just as busy as always!

Tiffiny: Really? I tried calling you yesterday after my Korean class. __________ (not) you home?

Michelle: Sorry, I __________ (not). I was at the gym, followed by a bike ride near the river.

Tiffiny: That's okay. I just thought we could have a catch-up over coffee. __________ your gym session and bike ride good?

Michelle: Ah… they __________ (not) that good. The gym was busy and there __________ (not) any energy drinks left in the vending machine! Anyway, tell me about what you've been up to? __________ you away somewhere nice at the weekend?

Tiffiny: Haha! No, I __________ (not). We __________ at my husband's family in Busan.

Michelle: And that __________ (not) fun?

Tiffiny: No, it was terrible! We __________ (not) able to relax at all.

Exercise 5 *Talking about the Past: Complete the following sentences using the past simple form of the verb.*

1.	cook	I __________ dinner at home yesterday. I __________ (not) dinner at home yesterday. __________ I __________ dinner at home yesterday? Yes, you __________ . / No, you __________ .
2.	play	He __________ soccer with his friends at the weekend. He __________ (not) soccer with his friends at the weekend. __________ he __________ soccer with his friends at the weekend? Yes, he __________ . / No, he __________ .

3.	work	They ________ all day on their homework. They ________ (not) all day on their homework. ________ they ________ all day on their homework? Yes, they ________ . / No, they ________ .
4.	empty	We ________ the trash after breakfast yesterday. We ________ (not) the trash after breakfast yesterday. ________ we ________ the trash after breakfast yesterday? Yes, we ________ . / No, we ________ .
5.	go	She ________ home after school. She ________ (not) home after school. ________ she ________ home after school? Yes, she ________ . / No, she ________ .
6.	eat	It ________ meat for its meal. It ________ (not) meat for its meal. ________ it ________ meat for it meal? Yes, it ________ . / No, it ________ .
7.	see	He ________ a baseball game with his friends. He ________ (not) a baseball game with his friends. ________ he ________ a baseball game with his friends? Yes, he ________ . / No, he ________ .

Exercise 6 *Look at the following table, before answering in FULL SENTENCES. (Use verbs in their past tense form)*

	Last weekend	Day before yesterday	Yesterday
Marco	eat pizza	take a nap	go swimming
P.K.	go food shopping	go to Korean class	get ready for school (a.m.)
Wei Zhang	eat Turkish food	go to English academy	sleep until 12:00

1. Did Marco go shopping last weekend?

____.

2. Did Marco go swimming the day before yesterday?

____.

3. Did P.K. have Korean class the day before yesterday?

____.

4. Did Wei Zhang eat French food last weekend?

____.

5. Did Wei Zhang sleep until 10:00 yesterday?

____.

Exercise 7 *Complete the following profile using the Past Simple, Present Simple, and Present Continuous tenses.*

Erica is from the U.S.A. She ______________ (live) in Seoul, South Korea. Erica ______________ (be) born on January 16, 1995. Before becoming a student, she ______________ (be) as a cashier in GAP. In her free time, Erica ______________ (help) her grandparents with housework and ______________ the laundry. On the weekend, you can find Erica ______________ (play) golf, ______________ (shop) and ______________ (eat) out. Last weekend, she ______________ (go) to a spa for the day on Saturday. Yesterday, Erica ______________ (do) homework and ______________ (have) coffee with classmates.

Exercise 8 *Use the words "Let's", "Should", and "Could" to answer the following questions. Sometimes there is more than one answer.*

1. What do you want to do today?

____.

2. Where should we go on vacation?

____.

3. When do you want to meet next time?

____.

NEW GRAMMAR: Correlative Conjunctions:

Correlative conjunctions are pairs of conjunctions that link words, phrases or clauses.

BOTH / AND, EITHER / OR and NEITHER / NOR

BOTH	A AND B	(A B)	• I like **both** *comedies* and *dramas*. • She is going to **both** *work* **and** *university* everyday.
EITHER	A OR B, not two	(A) ~~B~~	• I want to go to **either** *Malaysia* or *Thailand* this summer.
		~~A~~ (B)	• For lunch? I'll have **either** the *chef salad* **or** the *caesar salad*.
NEITHER	Not A and not B	~~A~~ ~~B~~	• Would you like a *ham* or *beef* sandwich? **Neither.** I don't eat meat. I am a vegetarian. **Neither** *Tuesday* **nor** *Wednesday* was available for the meeting.

1. ________ the time nor the place is acceptable for the boss. I'm sorry.
   A) Both B) Either C) Neither
2. I take ________ milk and sugar in my coffee, please.
   A) Both B) Either C) Neither
3. What day is it today, the 4th or the 5th? ________ . It is the 6th today.
   A) Both B) Neither C) Either
4. When should I call you, morning or afternoon?
   ________ is fine. I'm around all day tomorrow.
   A) Both B) Neither C) Either
5. Yesterday, the two dogs ________ in a fight but neither ________ hurt.
   A) were / was B) was / was C) is / is D) are / are
6. A: Can I have something to drink?
   B: Sure. Would you like either juice ________ soda?
   A) and B) or C) nor D) both

7. It's raining today. You can ________ go home or go to the school.

A) either B) both C) neither

8. I like ________ comedies and action movies.

A) either B) both C) neither

9. Do you want to watch a movie or play a board game?

________! Let's go for a walk.

A) either B) both C) neither

10. A: I could go for a nice pizza right now.

B: Yeah. Either that ________ a hamburger.

A) and B) nor C) or

11. Neither the fisherman ________ his wife was very happy.

A) and B) nor C) or

12. Both of the friends ________ very tired after studying all right.

A) is B) was C) were

13. Either it's really hot in here ________ I have a fever.

A) and B) nor C) or

14. Neither of the fishermen ________ any fish yesterday.

Both of the fishermen ________ angry.

A) catched / were B) caught / was

C) caught / were D) catched / was

UNIT 6 Shopping

Warm-up Questions:

16. What is your daily routine?

I ______________ every day.
(verb)

DAILY ROUTINE:
Every day, I wake up at 6:00 a.m.
I take a shower and get dressed. I make coffee. I drink coffee and eat toast for breakfast. Then I go to work. I work until 6 p.m. and then I go home and rest.

"Need to" and "Want to":
Both need "to" and a verb WITHOUT "ING".

I need to eat. ✔ I need to eating. ✘
I want to rest. ✔ I want to resting. ✘

"Want" and "Need" are part of a category of verb that requires the infinitive form. These verbs tend to be "mental" verbs.

– agree to (verb) – decide to (verb)
– forget to (verb) – hope to (verb)
– plan to (verb) – promise to (verb)
– try to (verb) – remember to (verb)

17. What things do you need to do every day?

I need to ______________ every day.
(verb)

18. What things do you want to do every day?

I want to ______________ every day.
(verb)

Dialogue A: *"Shopping with Dad"*

Cashier: Hello again. 1. Is there anything I can help you with today?

Mr. Park: Thanks but we're just 2. looking today.

Erica: Hey, Dad. Which dress do you think is nicer?

Mr. Park: I don't know. Which one 3. is the cheapest?

Erica: You are the cheapest.

Mr. Park: That may be true, but I still need to know which of these will cost me the least.

Cashier: The blue one is the cheapest one, but I don't think it is the prettiest. Not for your daughter anyway. I think she needs something a bit darker.

Mr. Park: I like the blue one. Blue is my favorite color.

Erica: Come on, Dad. Blue's the ugliest one. That is why it's the cheapest. 4. Which one would make me look best?

Cashier: Why not try on these two? We'll see which one is the best match. This white one is bigger than the black one. If it is too big for you, I will try to find a smaller one in the back of the store. However, black is slimming.

Mr. Park: Black! It's a dance, not a funeral.

Cashier: It's certainly not a funeral dress. It is quite short and has a low neckline.

Mr. Park: How short are we talking?

Erica: 5. Ignore him. He is a typical father.

Cashier: Did you decide which you would like to try on?

Erica: Give me them both. Where can I try them on?

Cashier: Right over there.

Substitution Drill: Use the following responses in the above conversation.

		A. FORMAL	B. INFORMAL
1.	Is there anything I can help you with today?	What can I help you with?	Do you need any help?
2.	looking today.	comparing prices.	window shopping.
3.	is the cheapest?	has the lowest price?	costs the least?
4.	Which one would make me look best?	Which one do you think would look best on me?	What do you have that would make me look gorgeous?
5.	Ignore him!	I wouldn't worry about what he says!	Don't listen to him!

Conversation Corner 1: *How to talk while shopping.*

Talk with a partner. C ➡ clerk, S1 ➡ Shopper 1, S2 ➡ Shopper 2

S1: Which one looks better?
S2: I like the blue one. It brings out your eyes.

S1: How much is this?
C: The total will be 40 dollars.

S1: Which is the cheapest?
C: That one. It's only 20 dollars.

S1: Do you have a smaller size?
C: Yes, this one's smaller.
or
C: No, that is the smallest size we have for that item.

S1: Can I get a refund?
C: Yes, do you have the receipt?
or
C: I'm sorry but there are no refunds. All sales are final.

S1: Can I exchange this for a different color?
C: Yes. What color would you like?
or
C: Sorry, we don't do exchanges.

C: And how would you like to pay today?
S1: Do you take credit cards?
or
S2: I'll pay by cash.

S2: Can you help me pick out a gift for my daughter?
C: Sure. What kinds of things does your daughter like?
or
C: Certainly. What did you have in mind?

C: Thank you for shopping with us today. Do you want your receipt?
S1: Yes, sure. Put it in the bag.
or
S2: No, thanks. You can throw it away.

Grammar Gallery 1: *Comparatives*

Which shirt is **smaller**?	The black shirt is **smaller than** the white shirt.
Which shirt is **more expensive**?	The white shirt is **more expensive** than the black shirt.

Use comparatives when you are comparing two things.

Exercise 1 *Use these rules to make comparatives*

	One syllable (1음절)	
small ➡ small**er than** cheap ➡ cheap**er than** large ➡ large**r**	1. old ➡ *older than*	2. young ➡
	3. short ➡	4. tall ➡
	One syllable ends with vowel + consonant	
big ➡ bi**gger than** thin ➡ thi**nner than**	5. fat ➡ *fatter than*	6. sad ➡
	7. hot ➡	8. red ➡
	ends with y	
happ**y** ➡ happ**ier than** prett**y** ➡ prett**ier than**	9. hungry ➡ *hungrier than*	10. easy ➡
	11. ugly ➡	12. heavy ➡
	Two or more syllables (2음절 이상)	
expensive ➡ **more** expensive **than** (**less** expensive **than**) beautiful ➡ **more** beautiful **than** (**less** beautiful **than**)	13. difficult ➡ ***more*** difficult ***than***	
	14. flexible ➡	
	15. suitable ➡	
	16. famous ➡	
	irregular (불규칙)	
good ➡ **better than** bad ➡ **worse than**	17. far ➡ farther than / further than	
	18. quiet ➡	
	19. fun ➡	
	20. little ➡	

Exercise 2 *Fill in the blanks using the picture provided.*

1. Which car is bigger? The black car is bigger than the white car.
2. Which car is smaller? The ______ car is smaller than the ______ car.
3. Which car is larger? The black car is ______ ______ the ______ ______ .
4. Which car is cheaper? The ______ ______ is ______ ______ the ______ ______ .
5. Which car is more expensive? The black car is ______ ______ ______ the white car.
6. Which car is less expensive? ________________________ .

Your thoughts: Which car would you like to buy? Why?

________________________ .

You can use superlatives when you compare three or more things.

NOTE: A superlative will always have a "the" because "the" means there is "only one"

Grammar Gallery 2: Superlatives

Exercise 3 *Use the rules to make superlatives.*

One syllable (1음절)		
small → smaller → the smallest cheap → cheaper → the cheapest large → larger → the largest	1. old → *the oldest*	2. smart →
	3. young →	4. fast →
	5. short →	6. new →
One syllable ends with vowel + consonant		
big → bigger → the biggest thin → thinner → the thinnest	7. fat → *the fattest*	8. wet →
	9. sad →	10. red →
	11. hot →	12. flat →

ends with y	
happy ➡ happier ➡ the happiest pretty ➡ prettier ➡ the prettiest	13. hungry ➡ *the hungriest*
	14. ugly ➡
	15. heavy ➡
Two or more syllables (2음절 이상)	
expensive ➡ more expensive ➡ the most expensive less expensive ➡ the least expensive	16. beautiful ➡ *the most beautiful*
	17. suitable ➡
	18. difficult ➡
irregular (불규칙)	
good ➡ better ➡ the best bad ➡ worse ➡ the worst	19. far ➡ *the farthest / the furthest*
	20. quiet ➡
	21. fun ➡
	22. little ➡

Exercise 4 *Fill in the blanks.*

	Which shirt is **the smallest?**
	Which shirt is **the most expensive?**
	Is the yellow shirt **the smallest?**
	Is the purple shirt **the most expensive?**

1. Which shirt is the smallest? The yellow shirt is the smallest.
2. Which shirt is the biggest? The ________ shirt is ________ ________ .
3. Which shirt is the cheapest? ________ ________ ________ is the cheapest.
4. Which shirt is the least expensive? ________________________________ .
5. Which shirt is the largest? ________________________________ .

Your thoughts: Which shirt would you like to buy? Why?

____ .

Exercise 5 *Make the comparative and superlative adjectives:*

	Comparative (비교급)	**Superlative** (최상급)
funny		
hard		
colorful		
long		
friendly		
common		
fantastic		
wise		
moody		

Exercise 6 *Use this chart to answer the questions. Write "a", "b" or "c".*

	A	**B**	**C**
 A B C	$750 size: 140 cm	$500 size: 120 cm	$350 size: 90 cm
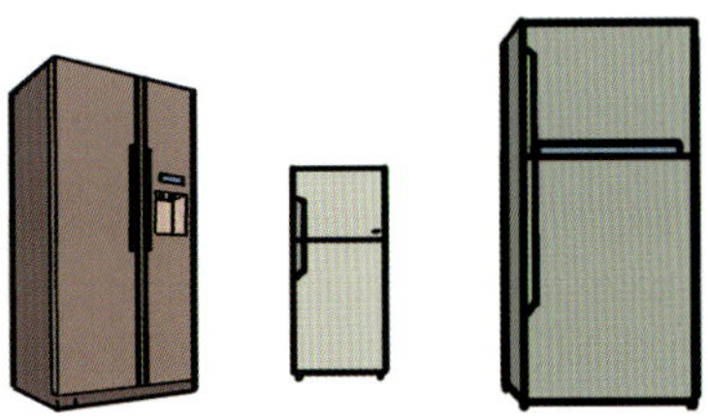 A B C	$1,500 weight: 100kg	$750 weight: 70 kg	$1,000 weight: 110kg

1. Which T.V. is the cheapest? __________

2. Which T.V. is the most expensive? __________

3. Which T.V. is the largest? __________

4. Which refrigerator is the cheapest? __________

5. Which refrigerator is the most expensive? __________

6. Which refrigerator is the heaviest? __________

7. Which T.V. would you buy? __________

   Why? ____.

8. Which refrigerator would you buy?

   Why? ____.

Exercise 7 *Multiple Choice: Choose the best answer from the choices below. Use the chart above:*

1. T.V. A is __________ than T.V. B.

   A) bigger B) the biggest C) biger D) smaller

2. T.V. C is __________ than T.V. B.

   A) bigger B) the smallest C) the bigger D) smaller

3. T.V. C is __________ .

   A) the most small B) the smaller C) smaller than D) the smallest

4. Refrigerator B is __________ .

   A) the heaviest B) the lightest C) the lighter D) lighter than

5. Refrigerator A is __________ Refrigerator B.

   A) heavier than B) heaviest than C) heavyer than D) the heaviest

6. Refrigerator A is __________ than Refrigerator C.

   A) cheaper than B) more expensive than C) expensiver than D) heavier than

Dialogue B: *"My Ice Cream Cone!"*

Mrs. Clark: I was waiting for you on Sullivan Street. Where were you?

Kevin: I was waiting in "What-A-Burger".

Mrs. Clark: You were what? What were you doing in there?

Kevin: I was 1. exchanging my empty ice cream cone for a new one. And I succeeded, at least in a way.

Mrs. Clark: Why was it empty? Did you eat it?

Kevin: It was on the floor.

Mrs. Clark: What was it doing on the floor?

Kevin: Andy was 2. horsing around and he hit my hand. The ice cream cone fell on the floor.

Mrs. Clark: Was he running around 3. without looking where he was going?

Kevin: Yeah.

Mrs. Clark: So what happened next?

Kevin: Well, I was explaining why it was melting on the ground, but the cashier was just 4. giving me the run around. He said that I had to show him a receipt. I had just bought it from him!

Mrs. Clark: I think I had better go and talk to him for you.

Kevin: It's O.K. mom. While I was talking to the clerk, the man behind me offered to buy me another ice cream cone. But I looked at the time and I saw that 5. I was running late to meet you. So I got a coupon for a free ice cream cone later.

Mrs. Clark: You are a clever little boy. Now, let's go. You were right. We are running late.

Substitution Drill: Use the following responses in the above conversation.

		A. FORMAL	B. INFORMAL
1.	exchanging my empty ice cream cone for a new one	returning my cone for a new one	giving my cone back to get a new one
2.	horsing around	roughhousing	playing roughly
3.	without looking where he was going?	and not paying attention?	blindly?
4.	giving me the run around.	giving me excuses.	talking a lot but not helping.
5.	I was running late to meet you.	I was late for our meeting.	I wasn't going to be on time to meet you.

Grammar Gallery 3: *Past Continuous*

RULE #1: SPECIFIC TIME IN THE PAST:

"Yesterday" is not specific and we use past simple for it.

Ex. I played soccer yesterday.

"Yesterday at 6:30 p.m." is specific time and we use "was / were" + "(verb)ing" for this form. This is called the past continuous.

Ex. I was playing soccer yesterday at 6:30 p.m.

Q: What were you doing last night at 9:00?
A: I was baking a cake.

Q: What were you doing after dinner last night?
A: I was reading a book.

Q: What were you doing in China last year?
A: I was hiking on the Great Wall.

RULE #2: 2 LONG ACTIONS AT THE SAME TIME IN THE PAST USING "WHILE"

6:30 p.m.: John playing soccer / Bobby taking a test

John was playing soccer while Bobby was taking a test

Q: What was Jenny doing while we were playing soccer?
A: She was drinking coffee and relaxing. She doesn't like to watch soccer.

Mark was watching T.V. while Paul and Molly were watching a movie. *or* Paul and Molly were watching a movie while Mark was watching T.V.

Q: What were you thinking while you were hanging there waiting for help?
A: I was thinking that this is my last time hiking... forever!

RULE #3: LONG ACTION / 1 SHORT ACTION NEAR THE SAME TIME (PAST) USING "WHILE" and "WHEN"

6:30 p.m.: John reading a book / phone rings

John was reading when the phone rang. / The phone rang while John was studying.

When the phone rang, John was studying. / While John was studying, the phone rang.

"When" is used with short action (past simple).

"While" is used with long action (past continuous.)

Timothy fell off the ladder while painting the ceiling.

Sarah was taking a shower when the delivery man knocked.

I saw George while driving to work yesterday.

Pronoun	Affirmative	Negative(Not)	Question
I He She It	I was eating dinner. He was eating... She was eating... It was eating...	I wasn't eating dinner. He wasn't eating... She wasn't eating... It wasn't eating... **(wasn't = was not)**	Was I eating last night at 6:00? Was he eating ...? Was she eating...? Was it eating...?
You We They	You were eating dinner. We were eating... They were eating...	You weren't eating dinner. We weren't eating... They weren't eating... **(weren't = were not)**	Were you eating last night at 6:00? Were we eating...? Were they eating...?

Exercise 8 *Fill in the blanks. Use "was" or "were" and the verb in the parentheses (　　).*

1. He ____________ (sleep) during the first class.
2. You ____________ (go) when it happened.

3. She ______________ (play) games at 7:00.

4. I ______________ (take) a bath when you called.

5. The team ______________ (play) well, but then the best player had his hand hurt.

6. We ______________ (wait) for the bus for 20 minutes.

7. Judy ______________ (dance) last night at 10.

8. Joe and Tom ______________ (eat) at noon.

9. We ______________ (hike) when it started raining.

10. I ______________ (study) while she ______________ (do) nothing. It is not fair.

Exercise 9 *What were they doing last night at 6:00 p.m.?*

	1.
	2.
	3.
	4.

	5.
	6.

Exercise 10 *Change the answers to "Past Continuous".*

1. What were you doing last night at 5:00?

   ~~I ate dinner.~~ *I was eating dinner.*

2. What were we doing Friday night?

   ~~We danced at a club.~~ ______________________________ .

3. What was he doing yesterday at noon?

   ~~He fixed his bicycle.~~ ______________________________ .

4. Where were they vacationing in 2013?

   ~~They vacationed in Australia.~~ ______________________________ .

5. Who was she dating last year?

   ~~She dated a soldier.~~ ______________________________ .

6. Why was the boy running away?

   ~~He hid from his friends.~~ ______________________________ .

7. What was she doing while I was shopping?

   ~~She sat in that chair the whole time.~~ ______________________________ .

8. Why was the team losing after halftime?

   ~~Because the other team played better.~~ ______________________________ .

9. What were you doing when you had your foot hurt?

   ~~I danced when I fell down.~~ ______________________________ .

10. What were you doing when I called?

    ~~I showered at that time.~~ ______________________________ .

Exercise 11 *Talk with your classmates about the past. Use "Past Continuous" and write the answers.*

Question	Your Answer	Partner's Answer
What were you doing at 7:00?	*I was ________ ing.*	
What were you doing at 9:00?		
What were you doing at midnight?		
What were you doing last Saturday at 4 p.m.?		
What were you doing this morning at 6:30 a.m.?		
What were you doing this morning at 8:30 a.m.?		
What were you doing last Saturday at 8:30 p.m.?		

Phrasal Verbs using "COME" and "CUT":

Phrasal Verb	Meaning	Example
come in	**a.** to join at a specific time. (특정한 시기에 합류하다.) **b.** to finish a race in a specific position. (특정한 순위로 경주를 마치다.)	**a.** This is when I came in to the meeting. **b.** She came in the 1st place.
come together	**a.** to meet. (만나다.) **b.** to start to work well together (잘 하기 시작하다.)	**a.** The flash mob came together at 1:00. p.m. **b.** After rehearsal, the band really came together.
come down with	**a.** to get sick (아프다.) **b.** to travel together (함께 여행하다.)	**a.** She came down with the flu. **b.** She came down to New York with Susan.

come across	**a.** to find something unexpected while doing something else. (뭔가를 하다가 예기치 못한 것을 발견하다.)	**a.** While walking to work, I came across my stolen car.
cut down	**a.** to cut something until it falls down (베어내다) **b.** to reduce (단축하다.)	**a.** He cut down the tree. **b.** He cut down on his eating, and lost weight.
cut in	**a.** to cheat in line; to steal someone's place (새치기하다.)	**a.** The car cut into traffic and caused an accident.
cut something out	**a.** to stop doing something (그만두다.)	**a.** Hey kids, cut it out or I'll send you to bed early.

Exercise 12 *Match the phrasal verbs with the pictures.*

1.

2.

3.

4.

5.

6.

7.

8.

TOEIC VOCABULARY

Read the following common TOEIC words. Memorize so that you can do well on the TOEIC. Write the Korean and English in the space below two times to help you learn.

Fluctuation: 변동, 파동.
Oil prices are subject to fluctuation for complex reasons.
유가는 복잡한 이유 때문에 요동치기 쉽다.

________ / ________ ________ / ________

Formal: 공식적인.
The staff say there is no formal structure for negotiating pay increases.
직원들은 급여 인상을 협의하기 위한 공식적인 조직이 없다고 합니다.

________ / ________ ________ / ________

Free of charge: 무료의.
All these services are available to the public free of charge.
이 모든 서비스는 대중에게 무료로 제공됩니다.

________ / ________ ________ / ________

Frequent: 빈번한.
At the bus terminal, buses depart and arrive at frequent intervals.
버스 터미널에서 버스들이 빈번한 시차를 두고 출발하고 도착한다.

________ / ________ ________ / ________

Frustrate: 좌절시키다.
The fact that he's working with amateurs really frustrates him.
비전문가들과 함께 일한다는 사실이 그를 정말 좌절시킨다.

________ / ________ ________ / ________

Fury: 격노.
The secret was leaked to the press, much to the president's fury.
비밀이 언론에 새어나가는 바람에 대통령이 매우 격노했다.

________ / ________ ________ / ________

Gaseous: 기체의.
The toxic materials spread all over the region in a gaseous form.
독성 물질들이 기체 형태로 사방으로 퍼져나갔다.

________ / ________ ________ / ________

Generate: 발생시키다.
The program would generate a lot of new jobs.
이번 계획이 많은 신규 일자리를 창출할 것이다.

________ / ________ ________ / ________

Grant: 허가하다, 보조금.
The council has granted him permission to build on the site.
시의회는 그에게 그 곳에 건축할 수 있는 허가를 내 주었다.
Anyone wishing to apply for a grant should submit an application.
보조금을 신청하려는 사람은 누구나 신청서를 제출해야 한다.

________ / ________ ________ / ________

Hazard: 위험.
Polluted air and water are a hazard to anyone.
오염된 공기와 물은 누구에게라도 위험이다.

________ / ________ ________ / ________

Illegible: 읽을 수 없는.
What she wrote on the contract is totally illegible.
그녀가 계약서에 기재한 내용은 전혀 읽을 수가 없다.

________ / ________ ________ / ________

Immediately: 즉시.
He retired immediately after the end of the war.
그는 전후 즉시 퇴직했다.

________ / ________ ________ / ________

Impact: 영향, 충격.
We need to assess the impact of the wildfire in Canada on climate change.
캐나다의 산불이 기후 변화에 끼치는 영향을 평가할 필요가 있다.

________ / ________ ________ / ________

Implement: 도입하다.
We have decided to implement the new safety regulations.

우리는 새로운 안전규정을 도입하기로 결정했다.

_______ / _______ _______ / _______

Implication: 암시, 내포된 의미.
The upcoming election will have profound implications for the future of U.S. politics.
다가오는 선거는 미국 정치의 미래에 심오한 의미를 지닐 것이다.

_______ / _______ _______ / _______

Impose: 부과하다.
Kenyan government imposed a ban on the sale of ivory.
케냐 정부는 상아 판매를 금지했다.

_______ / _______ _______ / _______

Impressive: 인상적인.
What the guest speaker said was so impressive.
초청연사의 연설이 매우 인상적이었다.

_______ / _______ _______ / _______

In charge of: 책임지고 있는.
The president put him in charge of the research team.
사장님은 그에게 연구팀을 맡겼다.

_______ / _______ _______ / _______

In particular: 특히.
It was a very good performance. I enjoyed the last act in particular.
매우 훌륭한 공연이었다. 특히 마지막 막이 좋았어.

_______ / _______ _______ / _______

In spite of: ~에도 불구하고.
She loved her husband in spite of the fact that he smoked too much.
남편이 과도한 흡연을 한다는 사실에도 불구하고 그녀는 남편을 사랑했다.

_______ / _______ _______ / _______

Out of stock: 재고가 없는.
I'm sorry but the swimsuit you are looking for is completely out of stock.
죄송한데 손님이 찾는 수영복은 전혀 재고가 없습니다.

_______ / _______ _______ / _______

Incentive: 자극, 보상금, 격려하는.
Cash awards provide an incentive for many people to improve their skills.
현찰로 상금을 주면 많은 이들이 자신의 기술을 향상시키도록 하는 자극이 된다.

_______ / _______ _______ / _______

Include: 포함하다.
Would you include a ruler on your list of essentials?
필수품 목록에 자도 포함시키시겠습니까?

_______ / _______ _______ / _______

Incur: 유발시키다.
You will be reimbursed for the damage incurred for the flaw of the product.
제품의 결정 때문에 발생된 피해에 대해 보상을 받게 될 겁니다.

_______ / _______ _______ / _______

Inflict: (피해를) 끼치다.
His negative statement inflicted serious damage on their relationship.
그의 부정적인 말이 그들의 관계에 심각한 피해를 끼쳤다.

_______ / _______ _______ / _______

Initiative: 솔선, 선창, 주도권, 추진력, 창의력
I wish my staff would show more initiative.
직원들이 보다 더 추진력을 발휘해 주기를 바란다.

_______ / _______ _______ / _______

Innovative: 혁신적인.
He has adopted innovative approaches to language teaching, such as CLT.
그는 언어 교육에 CLT와 같은 혁신적인 방식을 도입하였다.

_______ / _______ _______ / _______

Input: 투입, 의견.
Thank you for your input concerning the new plan.
새로운 계획에 관한 당신의 의견 감사 드립니다.

_______ / _______ _______ / _______

Inspire: 자극을 주다.
Inspired by what the boss said, I decided to resume the work.
사장님 말씀에 자극이 되어 업무를 재개하기로 결심했다.

_______ / _______ _______ / _______

Instance: 예.
They came across many instances of racial discrimination.
그들은 인종차별의 여러 가지 예를 마주하게 되었다.

_______ / _______ _______ / _______

UNIT

7 What a Night!

Review Questions:

1. What is your daily routine? (write 4 things you do every day.)

2. What is the most beautiful place you know?

Warm-up Questions:

Today's discussion is about skills and what you can do well.
This is common in a job interview (similar to "What are your strengths?").
Prepare your answer as if in a job interview.
That means choosing the best answer to represent a smart, talented employee.

19. What are you good at?

I'm good at ______________________________ .
(activity + ing)

What can you do well?

I can ______________________________ very well.
(verb) or (verb + noun)

20. What can your father do well? Mother?

My father can ______________________________ very well.
(verb) or (verb + noun)

My mother can ______________________________ very well.
(verb) or (verb + noun)

21. What do you want to be able to do in the future?

In the future, I want to be able to ______________________________ .
(activity)

ACTIVITIES TO BE "GOOD AT"

- **sports:** badminton, tennis, soccer, baseball etc.
- **studies:** English, math, history etc.
- **personal skills:** being friendly, communicating to others, working alone, helping others, listening to others etc.
- **creative skills:** writing, journaling, drawing, painting, cooking, baking.
- **odd but interesting:** solving... puzzles, crosswords, Sudoku, riddles etc.
  playing... cards, computer games etc.
- other: ______________________________

Why are these "good" and "bad" for job interview?

ACTIVITIES	
Good to mention at job interview	Bad to mention at job interview
• reading books • studying • taking tests • speaking English / Japanese / Chinese • ______________ • ______________	• watching T.V. • drinking alcohol with friends • dancing in Hongdae • sleeping • singing • ______________

Dialogue A: *"What a Night!"*

Michelle: So Marco, how was the date last night?

Marco: What a night! It was the worst first date ever.

Michelle: Why? 1. What went wrong?

Marco: What didn't go wrong is the better question.

Michelle: 2. Lay it on me, Marco. What happened?

Marco: It all started when I picked her up late because I was riding the wrong bus. So she started the date already angry. Then, I thought it would be nice to walk to the restaurant and 3. get to know each other. But while I was walking, I tripped on a hole in the sidewalk and fell. I ripped my jeans and hurt my knee.

Michelle: Wow. I am beginning to understand the kind of night you had. 4. Were you able to turn it around?

Marco: Not a chance. At the restaurant, I dropped my fork. When I was picking it up, I tripped the waiter. While he was trying not to fall down, he poured water all over my date. 5. She was so mad! I ended up walking her home in silence.

Michelle: I'm sorry to hear that Marco. I guess it wasn't meant to be.

Marco: You want to know the worst part?

Michelle: Worse than what already happened? What more could have gone wrong?

Marco: The worst part is I really felt a connection with her. And she was really cute.

Michelle: Oh, Marco. You are a hopeless romantic!

Substitution Drill: Use the following responses in the above conversation.

		A. FORMAL	B. INFORMAL
1.	What went wrong?	What was the problem?	When did things go south?
2.	Lay it on me,	Tell me what happened,	Tell me the story,
3.	get to know each other.	get familiar with each other.	learn about each other.
4.	Were you able to turn it around?	Were you able to change your luck?	Did things get better after that?
5.	She was so mad!	She was really angry!	She was furious!

Conversation Corner: At the Restaurant

Restaurant vocabulary: Match	
1. appetizer ______	a. a soup that is made for today only and changes every day
2. soup of the day ______	b. what the chef of the restaurant is selling that is not on the menu
3. today's special ______	c. main course of the meal, usually a meat
4. entrée ______	d. food that is served with the main course, usually potatoes or salad
5. sides ______	e. small dish of food to start the meal, often shared

Polite Requests / Offers:
Using "Would you...", "Could I..." are often the polite ways of asking for something or offering something.

Waiter:	**Customer:** (notice "can" because customer can be less polite)
Would you like more time before you order?	Can I get another glass of water?
Would you like to order an appetizer to start?	Can I get some more bread?
Could I bring you an appetizer to start?	Could we have some more time?
Could I get you something to drink?	Could you repeat the specials?
Would you like something to drink?	Can you recommend something?

With a partner, practice ordering from the sandwich menu. If you don't know what the sandwich is, use your cell phone to find a definition and image. Take turns being the waiter and the customer and practice ordering a meal.

(상대방과 함께 샌드위치 메뉴를 보고 주문하는 것을 연습해 보세요. 샌드위치가 무엇인지 모르시면 핸드폰을 이용해서 무엇인지 모습은 어떤지 확인해 보세요. 교대로 웨이터와 손님이 되어서 식사 주문을 연습해 보세요.)

JOE's

Sandwich Shop

* All sandwiches are served with one choice from the side menu.

Sandwiches:

Clubhouse Sandwich	$10.99
B.L.T. Sandwich	$ 8.99
Cheesesteak Sandwich	$12.99
Cuban Sandwich	$12.99
French Dip Sandwich	$10.99

Side Menu:

Chef Salad
Garden Salad
French Fries
Baked potato
Steamed vegetables

To Drink:

Soda	$1.50
Coffee	$1.00
Tea	$1.00
Milk	$1.00

Waiter: Good afternoon, are you ready to order?

Customer: Yes, what is the ________________ sandwich?

Waiter: It is ________________________________.

Customer: OK, I think I would like the ______________ sandwich with the ______________ on the side.

Waiter: Excellent choice. And would you like anything to drink?

Customer: Yes, I'd like a ________________.

Waiter: Fantastic! I will be right out with your drink.

Grammar Gallery 1: *Past Continuous Negative and Yes / No Questions*

Pronoun	Affirmative	Negative(Not)	Question
I He She It	I was eating dinner. He was eating... She was eating... It was eating...	I wasn't eating dinner. He wasn't eating... She wasn't eating... It wasn't eating... **(wasn't = was not)**	Was I eating last night at 6:00? Was he eating...? Was she eating...? Was it eating...?
You We They	You were eating dinner. We were eating... They were eating...	You weren't eating dinner. We weren't eating... They weren't eating... **(weren't = were not)**	Were you eating last night at 6:00? Were we eating...? Were they eating...?

Exercise 1 *Fill in the blanks. Use "wasn't" or "weren't" and the verb in the parentheses ( ).*

1. He __________ (sleep) during last class.
2. You __________ (go) home after school yesterday at 6:00.
3. She __________ (play) piano at 7:00.
4. I __________ (go) to school when you called.
5. The team __________ (play) well, but then the best player started to play better.
6. We __________ (wait) for the bus for long. It came right away.
7. Judy __________ (dance) last night at 10 p.m. She stayed home.
   She was feeling sick.
8. Joe and Tom __________ (eat) at noon.
9. We __________ (hike) when it started raining.
10. He __________ (study) while she __________ (wait) for him.

Exercise 2 *What were they doing last night at 6:00 p.m.?*

2 p.m. Yesterday NOT	2 p.m. Yesterday	
		**1.** He wasn't fishing yesterday at 2 p.m. He was working.
		2.
		3.
		4.
		5.
		6.

Exercise 3 *Yes / No questions and responses:*

1. Were you dancing (dance) at 8:00 p.m. last evening?

   No, I wasn't. I was studying (study).

2. ____________ he ____________ (work) while I was sleeping?

   Yes, ____________________.

3. ____________ they ____________ (have) a picnic at 10:00 a.m.?

   Yes, ____________________.

4. ____________ she ____________ (watch) a movie while I was sleeping?

   No, ____________. ____________________ (sleep)

5. ____________ she ____________ (play) piano when I called?

   Yes, ____________________.

6. ____________ we ____________ (study) at 9:00 p.m. last evening?

   No, ____________. ____________________ (eat)

7. ____________ you ____________ (exercise) this morning when I knocked?

   Yes, ____________________.

8. ____________ they ____________ (do) taekwondo when I was playing baseball?

   Yes, ____________________.

9. ____________ he ____________ (cook) dinner when the thief broke in?

   No, ____________. ____________________ (rest)

10. ____________ the dog ____________ (bark) last night after midnight?

    No, ____________. ____________________ (be) quiet.

11. ____________ John and Jim ____________ (bowl) last evening when I was working?

    Yes, ____________________.

12. ____________ the animals at the zoo ____________ (sleep) when the sun went down.

    No, ____________. ____________________ (eat)

Exercise 4 *With a partner, find out what they were doing last night at 7:30 p.m. Your partner can only answer "Yes, I was." or "No, I wasn't". Keep asking questions until you get the "Yes, I was." answer. Then let your partner ask you questions. Trade Partners.*

(상대방과 함께 어제 밤 7시 30분에 무엇을 하고 있었는지 확인해 보세요. 상대방은 "Yes, I was." 또는 "No, I wasn't."로만 답할 수 있습니다. "Yes, I was."라는 답을 들을 때까지 계속 질문하세요. 그런 뒤 상대방이 당신에게 질문을 하도록 해 보세요. 상대방을 바꾸어서 계속 연습해 보세요.)

Ex. A: Were you eating dinner? B: No, I wasn't.
A: Were you riding the bus? B: No, I wasn't.
A: Were you working part-time? B: No, I wasn't.
A: Were you going on a date? B: Yes, I was.

PARTNER 1	PARTNER 2
My partner was ______ ______	My partner was ______ ______
PARTNER 3	**PARTNER 4**
My partner was ______ ______	My partner was ______ ______
PARTNER 5	**PARTNER 6**
My partner was ______ ______	My partner was ______ ______

Exercise 5 *Look at the schedule and answer the questions below.*

Sarah's Schedule for last week							
	Saturday	Sunday	Monday	Tuesday	Wednesday	Thursday	Friday
morning 8 a.m.	sleep in late	sleep in late	cook breakfast	cook breakfast	cook breakfast	cook breakfast	cook breakfast
evening 7 p.m.	watch T.V. with family	eat out with family	cook dinner, do homework	cook dinner, do homework	cook dinner, do homework	do homework	cook dinner, do homework
evening 11 p.m.	watch T.V.	go to bed early	go to bed early	go to bed early	go to bed early	go to bed early	take a hot bath

1. Was Sarah going to bed early on Friday at 11 p.m.?

____.

2. Was Sarah going to bed early on Tuesday at 11 p.m.?

____.

3. Was Sarah cooking dinner on Wednesday at 7 p.m.?

____.

4. Was Sarah cooking breakfast on Wednesday at 8 a.m.?

____.

5. __________ Sarah __________ on Thursday at 7 p.m.? Yes, she was.
6. __________ Sarah __________ on Thursday at 11 p.m.? No, she wasn't.
7. __________ Sarah __________ on Saturday at 11 p.m.? Yes, she was.
8. __________ Sarah __________ on Monday at 8 a.m.? No, she wasn't.

Exercise 6 *6: Look at the schedule and answer the questions below.*

Joey and Beth's Schedule for last week							
	Saturday	Sunday	Monday	Tuesday	Wednesday	Thursday	Friday
morning 8 a.m.	hike a mountain	hike a mountain	go to work	go to work	go to work	go to work	go to work
evening 7 p.m.	camping outdoors	drive home	relax at home	go to Taekwon-do	relax at home	go to Taekwon-do	watch a movie
evening 11 p.m.	sleep in tent	go to bed early	watch TV	go to bed early	watch TV	go to bed early	have drinks

1. Were they going to bed early on Friday at 11 p.m.?

______________________.

2. Were they going to bed early on Tuesday at 11 p.m.?

______________________.

3. Were they cooking dinner on Wednesday at 7 p.m.?

______________________.

4. Were they cooking breakfast on Wednesday at 8 a.m.?

______________________.

5. __________ they __________ on Thursday at 7 p.m.? Yes, they were.
6. __________ they __________ on Thursday at 11 p.m.? No, they weren't.
7. __________ they __________ on Saturday at 11 p.m.? Yes, they were.
8. __________ they __________ on Monday at 8 a.m.? No, they weren't.

Dialogue B: *"At the Restaurant Again"*

Wei: This is my favorite Indian restaurant. I will finally get you that wonderful curry I promised you.

Erica: 1. I hope it was worth the wait and all the troubles.

Wei: Yes, I am still sorry you lost your job.

Erica: That's OK. I wasn't enjoying that job anyway. 2. I think I am better off. Now I can find a job that I enjoy more.

Wei: 3. That's the spirit! OK. Let's order!

Erica: How do you order? I don't recognize any of the words on this menu. There aren't any explanations.

Wei: I told you it was very authentic. I can ask for a different menu but if it's all right, I'll order for us both. I know this menu well.

Erica: Sure. 4. I trust your decision.

Wei: Biju, we're ready!

Biju: Good evening, Mr. Zhang. Nice to see you again. What would you like to order?

Wei: Hello again. I'd like those dumplings with potatoes and spices inside and that red curry with the lamb but not too spicy. 5. You know which one I'm talking about, right?

Biju: Of course. And how about the naan bread? Do you want any?

Wei: Of course! Garlic please! And could I get water with a twist of lemon to drink.

Erica: Same for me! Wow! That was some very impressive ordering!

Wei: Hey, I may not know what the names are, but I know what's tasty. You are in for a treat.

Substitution Drill: Use the following responses in the above conversation.

		A. FORMAL	B. INFORMAL
1.	I hope it was worth the wait	I hope it is as good as you have said.	I hope it is delicious.
2.	I think I am better off.	I think it is for the best.	I think it is a good thing.
3.	That's the spirit!	I like attitude.	Good thinking.
4.	I trust your decision.	I think you will choose correctly.	I believe you can do it.
5.	You know which one I'm talking about, right?	Do you remember which item I am referring to?	I think you know the one I like.

Grammar Gallery 2: *Past Continuous vs. Past Simple*

The main difference in "Past Continuous" and "Past Simple" lies in their USAGE. Many tests, including TOEIC, will take advantage of this fact. Study the table below carefully.
(과거진행 시제와 단순과거 시제의 주요한 차이점은 용례에 있습니다. 토익을 포함한 많은 시험에 많이 출제됩니다. 다음 도표를 잘 검토해 보세요.)

Past Simple	Past Continuous
used for actions in the past that are done and finished. (이미 수행되어 종료된 과거의 행동에 사용됨.) **Not specific / general time:** (특정한 시간이 아닌 일반적 시간) yesterday, last week, last month, two weeks ago, three years ago Ex. I played soccer yesterday.	used for actions in the past for three main specific times (3개의 주요한 특정한 시간대의 과거의 행위에 대해 사용됨.) **Specific Times:** a) Yesterday at (o'clock). (특정한 시간) I was playing soccer yesterday at 4 p.m. b) Yesterday "while" another long action was happening (오랜 시간에 걸친 다른 행위가 발생하는 동안의 과거 시간) I was playing soccer yesterday while you were studying. c) Yesterday "when" another short action happened (다른 짧은 시간에 걸친 행위가 발생한 과거.) I was playing soccer yesterday when it started to rain.

When mixing the Past Continuous and Past Simple, you need to follow two rules:

A) The past simple is the "short action", meaning that the action only takes a few seconds.
(단순과거 시제는 "짧은 행위" 즉 발생 시간이 몇 초에 걸쳐 발생하는 행위를 의미합니다.)

B) The past simple is usually after "when", and the past continuous is after "while".
(딘순과거 시제는 대개 "when" 뒤에 사용되고 과거진행 시제는 "while" 뒤에 종종 사용됩니다.)

Ex. I was showering <u>when</u> you called.
(was showering: Past Continuous; called: Past Simple)

<u>When</u> you called, I was showering.
(called: Past Simple; was showering: Past Continuous)

I called <u>while</u> you were showering.
(called: Past Simple; were showering: Past Continuous)

<u>While</u> you were showering, I called.
(were showering: Past Continuous; called: Past Simple)

Exercise 7 *Unscramble the sentence. Look at the examples on the previous page when using the " , ".*

(문장을 제대로 배열해 보세요. "comma"를 사용할 때에는 앞 페이지의 예를 살펴보세요.)

1. she / walking / , / While / they / was / called

   While she was walking, they called.

2. started / when / to / rain / They / sitting / were / outside / it

   ______________________________.

3. they / While / dancing / they / , / fell / were

   ______________________________.

4. phone / The / while / we / rang / T.V. / watching / were

   ______________________________.

5. while / He / they / shopping / were / dropped / wallet / his

   ______________________________.

6. was / came / they / in / Who / sleeping / ? / when

   ______________________________.

7. doing / were / yesterday / ? / 3:00 p.m. / What / you / at

   ______________________________.

8. waiting / he / you / were / , / While / woke up /

   ______________________________.

Exercise 8 *Fill in the blanks with the "Past Continuous" (was / were verb +ing) or "Past Simple" (ex. eat ate, walk walked). Note, some sentences may only need "Past Simple" and some only need "Past Continuous". Look at the clues and think carefully.*

(과거진행 시제 또는 단순과거 시제를 사용하여 다음의 빈 칸을 채워 보세요. 어떤 문장은 단순과거 시제만 사용할 수 있고 어떤 문장은 과거진행 시제만을 사용할 수 있다는 점에 주의하세요. 힌트를 보시고 잘 생각해 보세요.)

1. What __________ you __________ (do) when Lucy __________ (knock) on your door?
2. They __________ (sit) in a coffee shop when you __________ (call).

3. You __________ (arrive) at the party while __________ (talk) to my boss.

4. While Susie __________ (watch) a film, she __________ (fall) asleep.

5. Yesterday I __________ (go) to the library when I __________ (meet) Julie for a coffee.

6. While I __________ (play) basketball, I __________ (hurt) my ankle.

7. What __________ they __________ (do) at 10 p.m. last night?

   It __________ (be) really noisy.

8. Where __________ you __________ (go) last night when I __________ (see) you?

9. Who __________ he __________ (talk) to while I __________ (wait)?

   He __________ (not talk) to anyone. His battery on his phone was dead.

10. Yesterday, I was busy. First, I __________ (go) to my fitness club and __________ (exercise). Then, I __________ (have) to go shopping.

    While I __________ (shop), I __________ (see) my ex-girlfriend. What a day!

11. While she __________ (read) a magazine, the ground __________ (start) shaking.

    It was an earthquake.

12. I'm sorry I __________ (surprise) you. I didn't know you __________ (sleep) at 10 a.m. yesterday.

Exercise 9 *Fill in the incomplete sentences about yourself. Make some answers true and some answers false. Then share with a partner and have him or her guess true or false.*
(본인에 대한 불완전한 문장을 완성해 보세요. 어떤 답변은 옳게 만들고 어떤 답변은 틀리게 만들어 보세요. 그리고 나서 상대방과 공유하고 참인지 거짓인지 맞춰 보게 하세요.)

Ex. Yesterday at 9 p.m., I was at home studying.

Partner: I think that is false.

Yesterday at 9 p.m., I ______________________________________ .

Last Saturday at 12.pm., I ______________________________________ .

I ____________________ while the teacher was talking.

While I was coming to class this morning, ______________________________ .

I ____________________ at 1 a.m. last night.

Phrasal Verbs using "GIVE" and "GROW":

Phrasal Verb	Meaning	Example
give up	a. to quit, to stop doing something (포기하다.)	a. I give up on this homework. It is impossible.
give out	a. to hand somebody / somebodies a thing or things (나누어 주다.)	a. They are giving out free pizza at the school. Let's go.
give in / into	a. to surrender, to stop trying (항복하다, 그만두다.)	a. I gave into my hunger and ate a whole pizza. My diet is ruined.
give off	a. to make something, usually a bad smell or strange light (내뿜다.)	a. The weird machine was giving off a strange light and an odd cloud.
grow on	a. to start to like something you didn't like before (좋아지다.)	a. At first, I hated some of the K-pop music. But now it is growing on me.
grow up	a. to become more mature / closer to adult behaviour (성숙하다.)	a. He is growing up so fast. Soon, he will be in high school.
grow out of	a. to become too big for, or to become too mature for something you liked when younger (성숙하여 벗어나다.)	a. I used to love watching animated movies from Japan, but I grew out of them. Now they seem so childish.
grow apart	a. to stop having strong emotions of love for a person (멀어지다.)	a. He was my best friend until we went to different universities. I guess we grew apart, because I don't talk to him anymore.

Exercise 10 *Fill in the blanks with the correct phrasal verb from the list above. Use the correct tense as it is given in parentheses (   ).*

1. I'm sorry, Heather. I'm not interested in going to the amusement park.

   I ______________ (past simple) of enjoying those rides years ago.

2. Is he OK tonight? He ______________ (present continuous) a weird vibe.

3. A: You look terrible! Are you OK?

   B: I ______________ (present continuous) smoking.

   The first few days are the hardest.

4. OK. I ______________ (present simple). We can watch the romantic comedy. Let's stop arguing.

5. I'm so angry. The teacher ______________ (past simple) our test scores and I did terribly. I should have studied.

6. A: What happened to you and Sarah?

   B: We broke up. She was always working and we never saw each other.

   I guess we just ______________ (past tense)

7. It's time to ______________ (present simple). I can't live with my parents and do nothing forever.

8. I used to be afraid of foreign food, but the Korean BBQ restaurants ______________ (present continuous) me. I can't wait to go again.

TOEIC VOCABULARY

Read the following common TOEIC words. Memorize so that you can do well on the TOEIC. Write the Korean and English in the space below two times to help you learn.

Eliminate: 제거하다.
Our team was eliminated in the first round.
우리 팀은 1차전에서 탈락했다.

_________ / _________ _________ / _________

Embrace: 포함하다.
This course embraces several different aspects of biology.
이 과목은 생물학의 다양한 분야를 담고 있다.

_________ / _________ _________ / _________

Enable: ~할 수 있게 하다.
Incheon International Airport plans to build a new runway to enable jumbo jets to land.
인천국제공항은 대형 여객기가 착륙할 수 있도록 하기 위해 새 활주로를 건설할 계획이다.

_________ / _________ _________ / _________

Encounter: 우연히 만나다.
The government has encountered strong opposition to its plans to raise income tax.
정부는 소득세 인상 계획에 대한 강력한 반대에 직면했다.

_________ / _________ _________ / _________

Enforcement: 집행.
Citizens should follow the rules and regulations regarding the law enforcement.
시민들은 법 집행에 관한 규칙과 규정을 따라야 한다.

_________ / _________ _________ / _________

Engage in: 종사하다.
Despite her reluctance, she had to be engaged in the election campaign.
내키지 않았지만 그녀는 선거운동에 종사해야만 했다.

_________ / _________ _________ / _________

Enlarge: 확대하다.
A good way to enlarge your vocabulary is to read a daily newspaper.
어휘력을 늘릴 수 있는 좋은 방법은 일간 신문을 읽는 것이다.

_________ / _________ _________ / _________

Entitle: 자격을 부여하다.
Membership acquired by paying dues entitles you to the quarterly journal.
회비 납부를 함으로써 회원이 되면 분기별 회보를 받아볼 수 있다.

_________ / _________ _________ / _________

Entrepreneur: 기업가.
Her dream has been to become an ambitious entrepreneur.
그녀의 꿈은 야망 있는 기업가가 되는 것이었다.

_________ / _________ _________ / _________

Estimate: 견적, 평가.
The final estimate puts annual sales at around 1 million dollars.
최종 평가를 해 보니 연말 매출액이 약 백만 불에 도달했다.

_________ / _________ _________ / _________

Evaluation: 평가.
We need to carry out a proper evaluation of every new employee.
모든 신입사원에 대해 적절한 평가를 수행해야 할 필요가 있다.

_________ / _________ _________ / _________

Eventually: 결국, 궁극적으로.
He eventually escaped and made his way back to his motherland.
그는 결국 탈출하여 고국으로 돌아갔다.

_________ / _________ _________ / _________

Examine: 검사하다, 조사하다.
A team of divers was sent down to examine the sunken submarine.
잠수부 한 팀이 침몰한 잠수함을 조사하기 위해 파견되었다.

_________ / _________ _________ / _________

Exceed: 초과하다.
Working hours must not exceed 37 hours a week in France.
프랑스에서는 주당 근로시간이 37시간을 초과할 수 없다.

_________ / _________ _________ / _________

Excel: 능가하다.
She excels other contestants in the technique and the expression of her emotion.
그녀는 기교와 감정표현에 있어서 다른 경쟁자들을 능가한다.

________ /________ ________ /________

Exceptionally: 예외적으로
He proved his alibi exceptionally well using some evidence.
그는 약간의 증거를 활용하여 자신의 알리바이를 아주 잘 증명하였다.

________ /________ ________ /________

Exempt: 면제되는, 면제하다, 면제자.
Children under the age of 7 are exempt from the entrance fee.
7세 미만의 어린이는 입장료 면제입니다.

________ /________ ________ /________

Expenditure: 지출.
Opposition leaders asked for huge cuts in the public sector expenditure.
야당 지도자들은 공공 부문 지출의 대규모 삭감을 요구했다.

________ /________ ________ /________

Experimental: 실험적인.
A hypothesis is tested by finding experimental evidence for it.
가설은 그에 대한 실험적 증거를 찾아야 증명된다.

________ /________ ________ /________

Expire: 종료되다.
The lease on my car expires on Jan. 22.
내 차의 임대는 1월 22일 종료된다.

________ /________ ________ /________

Extend: 늘이다, 계속하다.
Some majors in the university extend over two years.
대학의 몇몇 전공은 2년 이상 지속된다.

________ /________ ________ /________

Extremely: 매우, 극단적으로.
Even seismology experts feel it is extremely difficult to predict earthquakes.
지진학자조차도 지진을 예측하는 것은 매우 어렵다고 생각한다.
I'm extremely sorry to have troubled you.
귀찮게 해 드려 대단히 죄송합니다.

________ /________ ________ /________

Facility: 설비.
The hotel has its own pool and leisure facilities, let alone conference rooms.
호텔은 회의실은 말할 것도 없고 자체 수영장과 여가시설을 보유하고 있다.

________ /________ ________ /________

Failure: 실패.
The advertising campaign was a total failure.
이번 광고활동은 철저한 실패였다.

________ /________ ________ /________

Fairly: 꽤.
They have done the work fairly well.
그들은 작업을 꽤 잘 해냈다.

________ /________ ________ /________

Favorable: 호의적인.
Many Asian countries have a favorable attitude to Korea.
많은 아시아 국가는 한국에 호의적인 태도를 지니고 있다.
The disease spreads quickly under favorable conditions.
질병은 양호한 조건 하에서 급속히 퍼져나간다.

________ /________ ________ /________

Feature: 특징.
One of the distinguished features of modern banking is its dependence on computers.
현대 금융의 한 가지 두드러진 특징은 컴퓨터에 의존한다는 것이다.

________ /________ ________ /________

Feedback: 반응, 논평.
I always try to give each student some feedback on the task.
나는 학생들에게 항상 과제에 대해 논평을 해 주려고 한다.

________ /________ ________ /________

Finance: 금융.
Many people refuse to answer questions about their personal finances.
많은 이들이 자신의 개인적 금융상황에 대한 질문에 답하기를 거부한다.

________ /________ ________ /________

Fiscal: 재정상의
The government has difficulty overcoming a fiscal crisis.
정부는 재정 위기를 극복하느라 힘겨워하고 있다.

________ /________ ________ /________

UNIT

8 How Do I Use This?

Review Questions:

1. What do you want to be able to do in the future?

   In the future, I want to be able to ______________ .
   (activity)

2. What things do you need to do every day?

   I need to ______________ and ______________ every day.
   (verb) (verb)

3. What things do you want to do every day?

   I want to ______________ and ______________ every day.
   (verb) (verb)

Warm-up Questions:

22. What are you bad at? What can't you do well?

   I am bad at ______________ . I can't ______________ well.
   (activity) (activity)

23. What's your favorite kind of weather? Why?

My favorite kind of weather is ______________________________ .

(sunny / rainy / snowy / cloudy / foggy /etc.)

because ______________________________ .

(why you like that weather)

24. What is your favorite season? What do you do in that season?

My favorite season is ______________________________ .

(summer / fall / winter / spring)

because I can ______________________________ .

(what you can do in this season)

Conversation Corner: *Appropriate Small Talk*

Small talk is supposed to be casual and friendly, not controversial or personal. This can be in an elevator or while waiting in line. Please note: the washroom is not a place for small talk.

(잡담은 격식이 없이 친근하기 마련이어서 논쟁을 한다거나 사적인 내용을 나누지 않습니다. 엘리베이터 안에서나 줄을 서 있는 동안에도 가능합니다. 주의할 사항은 화장실은 적절한 장소가 아니라는 것입니다.)

Safe topics: (가능한 대화 주제)

- the weather
- recent movies
- current events
- nice comments about other person's clothes / fashion sense

Not safe topics: (피해야 할 대화 주제)

- personal information
- salary / money
- other person's body
- religion
- politics

Look at the following list of questions / topics.
Which are OK to talk to strangers about and which are not?
Put the numbers in the correct boxes below.

1. It's beautiful today, isn't it?	**2.** Is that your shirt with the weird colors and ugly picture?
3. So where are you going on vacation?	**4.** Where are you from?
5. Are you from around here?	**6.** What do you think about the U.S.A. President?
7. Are you a Christian?	**8.** Did you hear about the new market opening up near here?
9. How much money do you make?	**10.** I like your blouse. Is it new?
11. Where do you go to church?	**12.** Are you pregnant?
13. Do you think the rain will end soon?	**14.** Where do you work? Do they pay well?
15. Did you see the new Iron Man / Avengers movie?	**16.** How do you feel about death?
17. So… what kind of movies do you like?	**18.** Do you like to dance?
19. Are you into tattoos and piercings?	**20.** Did you hear that our local school is having a bake sale?
21. I think you need to exercise. Do you want me to recommend a gym?	**22.** Do you like men or women?

Appropriate (OK) ✔	**Inappropriate (not OK) ✘**
1.	2.

Dialogue A: *"How do you use this?"*

Wei: Hey Marco! I didn't know you did your laundry here?

Marco: Hey Wei! 1. I'm glad to see a friendly face. I've never been to a laundromat before. My washing machine broke down. Speaking of laundry, you certainly have a lot.

Wei: Yes. I have been working a lot lately and 2. haven't had time to do laundry.

Marco: I see. I'm just getting back from vacation so I have a few big loads of laundry as well. Are you going to use this machine?

Wei: 3. Nope. You go ahead. I'm putting stuff in the dryer.

Marco: Thanks. Oh…these machines take coins. Do you have any change?

Wei: I only have about a dollar, but there's a change machine over there.

Marco: Great. OK, next question. Wei, 4. could you show me how to use this machine? It won't take my money.

Wei: It's no problem. I have had problems with that thing before. So you said you went on a little vacation. Where did you go?

Marco: I went to Bali with some friends. It was amazing!

Wei: Wow. Sounds great but 5. I'm going to take off for a bit. Maybe we can talk about it after my clothes are dry when I come back.

Marco: Sure, but before you go, can you help me with the machine? There are a lot more buttons and options here than at home.

Substitution Drill: Use the following responses in the above conversation.

		A. FORMAL	B. INFORMAL
1.	I'm glad to see a friendly face.	It is good to see a familiar face.	It is nice to see someone I know.
2.	haven't had time to do laundry.	have gotten behind on the laundry.	have been too busy to do laundry.
3.	Nope. You go ahead.	No, I'm not. Feel free to use it.	No. It's all yours.
4.	could you show me how to use this machine?	could you tell me what to do to make this machine work?	could you help me with this machine?
5.	I'm going to take off for a bit.	I have to leave for a while.	I have to go out and come back later.

Grammar Gallery 1: *Future Tense "be going to (verb)"*

Pronoun	Affirmative	Negative	Question(?)
I	am going to (verb)	am not going to (verb)	Am I going to (verb)...?
You We They	are going to (verb)	are not going to (verb) aren't going to (verb)	Are you / we / they going to (verb)...?
He She It	is going to (verb)	is not going to (verb) isn't going to (verb)	Is he / she / it going to (verb)...?

Exercise 1 *Fill in the blanks with the correct form of "be going to (verb)".*

1. You ______________ (earn) a lot of money but ______________ (not be) happy with it.
2. He ______________ (travel) around the world before he ______________ (go) to university.
3. She ______________ (study) languages all over the world. She ______________ (meet) lots of interesting people.
4. Everybody ______________ (adore) you if you are kind and nice. But if you ______________ (not be) that way, please don't come to my party tomorrow.
5. I ______________ (not have) any problems in the near future.
6. Many people ______________ (buy) new cell phones next year.
7. She ______________ (help) you with your shopping next week.
8. There ______________ (not be) anything left to wish for.
9. Everything ______________ (be) perfect but first, you ______________ (work) hard.
10. You ______________ (not marry) until you are 30 years old, but you ______________ (be) very happy.

Exercise 2 *Use the correct form of "be going to (verb)" to finish the paragraphs about the future plans for the following people.*

1. Peter and Paul ____________ (go) to France next week. They ____________ (get up) very early and go to the airport. They ____________ (take) the bus because a taxi ____________ (cost) too much money. They ____________ (not go) by train, because the train ____________ (not be) there on time.
2. I ____________ (meet) my friend Sarah tomorrow. She ____________ (move) to Australia in a couple of weeks. She ____________ (work) there and she ____________ (not visit) me for the next 6 months. I've asked her: "____________ you ____________ (live) in Australia forever?" She answered: "No, of course not." I ____________ (miss) her.
3. James ____________ (marry) his girlfriend Lara next month. They ____________ (travel) to Japan for their honeymoon. They ____________ (not stay) very long though – only for 4 days. They ____________ (not spend) much money, either. The wedding was too expensive and they ____________ (have) a baby soon.

NOTE: Future with "will" and "be going to (verb)" are similar, but NOT the same. Many Second Language learners use "will" because it is easier, but it is not always correct.
("will"과 "be going to(동사원형)"를 사용하는 미래시제는 비슷하기는 하지만 같은 것이 아닙니다. 많은 영어 학습자들이 사용하기 편리한 "will"을 사용하기는 하지만 항상 옳은 것은 아닙니다.)

WILL (VERB)	BE GOING TO (VERB)
– used at the moment when decision is made (no plans have yet been made) 결정을 한 순간에 사용함 (아무런 계획도 세워진 것이 아님.) – used with predictions (weather, thoughts about future based on beliefs) 예측할 때 사용함 (믿음에 바탕을 두고 날씨나 미래에 대한 생각을 표현함.) – also used with promises or offers, and even threats 약속, 제안, 그리고 심지어 협박할 때에도 사용됨.	– used if decision has been made before now (plans have already been made) 이전에 결정된 사항에 대해 사용함 (계획이 이미 수립되어 있음.) – used based on evidence 증거에 바탕을 두고 사용함

Look at the following example.

What are you doing this weekend?

➡ I will watch a movie or hang out.

➡ I'm going to watch a movie with Sarah.
⬆
(has a plan already)

Exercise 3 *Use "will", "won't" or the correct form of "be going to (verb)" to complete the following sentences. In some cases, both forms might be acceptable.*

1. I ______________ join you this weekend. I don't think I have any other plans.
2. He ______________ give you a good present for your birthday.
   He has bought it already.
3. I think I ______________ go to the cinema when I finish my homework.
   I need a break.
4. A: I don't think it ______________ rain later today. It is too sunny.
   B: You are right. It ______________ stay sunny. There is not even one cloud in the sky.
5. A: Who can help Joey finish his homework?
   B: Beth ______________ . She promised to do that earlier.
6. I bought 2 tickets to the new action thriller.
   I ______________ ask Susie on a date later.
7. She ______________ help you with your homework. Don't worry!
8. Perhaps I ______________ borrow her car, if she lets me.
9. We ______________ visit you next month. I have made the travel plans.
10. He ______________ be tired tomorrow. He needs to study all night.

Exercise 4 *Talk with another student. Ask about his or her plans for the weekend and write the responses.*

PARTNER NAME	WEEKEND PLANS

Dialogue B: *"What are your weekend plans?"*

Marco: Hi, Michelle, where are you going to in such a rush?

Michelle: Oh, hi Marco. I'm going to go buy a new swimsuit for the party this weekend. Are you going to go to Bob's party this weekend?

Marco: Bob's end of the semester pool party? 1. Try to keep me away! I really need to let loose and have some fun. This semester has been so tough. Anyway, 2. I'm glad I caught you. What are you going to do later this afternoon after shopping?

Michelle: Hmm, this afternoon? I don't think I have any plans for later. Why?

Marco: Great. I'm going to help you pick out a nice swimsuit and then you are going to come to a movie with me later. I bought two tickets earlier but 3. my date bailed on me.

Michelle: Well, I guess that would be OK depending on two things.

Marco: What are the two things?

Michelle: One. The movie isn't a drama. I'm going to need some action tonight or I'll fall asleep. And two, you are going to buy me popcorn and a drink without complaining 4. about the rip-off cost.

Marco: 5. You drive a hard bargain. Agreed! I think that is worth it, especially if you are going to be my swimsuit model all afternoon.

Michelle: That's right. I think I should ask for more!

Substitution Drill: Use the following responses in the above conversation.

		A. FORMAL	B. INFORMAL
1.	Try to keep me away!	I'm definitely going to be there!	Try to stop me from coming!
2.	I'm glad I caught you.	I'm glad we met each other this way.	I'm glad we suddenly met.
3.	my date bailed on me.	my date cancelled on me.	my date can't make it.
4.	about the rip-off cost.	about the expensive price.	about the insanely high price.
5.	You drive a hard bargain.	You expect a lot in return.	You are asking for quite a bit.

Grammar Gallery 2: *Future Tense "be going to (verb)"*

Yes / No Question form and WWWWWH Questions

Pronoun	Affirmative	Negative	Question(?)
I	am going to (verb)	am not going to (verb)	Am I going to (verb)...?
You We They	are going to (verb)	are not going to (verb) aren't going to (verb)	Are you / we / they going to (verb)...?
He She It	is going to (verb)	is not going to (verb) isn't going to (verb)	Is he / she / it going to (verb)...?

Exercise 5 *Make Yes / No Questions then answer using P.K.'s schedule for next week.*

	Morning	Evening
Monday	go to college	visit mother
Tuesday	sleep in	play table tennis
Wednesday	clean the house with wife	watch football with Marco
Thursday	study English with James	go to the gym
Friday	stay in bed	go to the disco with wife

1. Is P.K. going to go to college on Monday morning? Yes, he is.
2. ________ he ________ sleep in on Thursday morning? ________ , he ________ .
   He ______________ study English on Thursday morning.
3. ________ P.K. and his wife ________ go to the disco on Friday night?
   ________ , they ________ .
4. ________ James ________ study English with P.K. on Wednesday?
   ________ , he ________ . He ______________ study English on Thursday.

5. ________ P.K. and Marco ________ watch football on Wednesday?

________ , they ________ .

6. ________ P.K. and Marco ________ watch football on Friday?

________ , they ________ . They ________ watch football on Wednesday.

7. ________ P.K. ________ visit his mother on Tuesday? ________ , he ________ .

He ____________ visit his mother on Monday.

8. ________ P.K. and his wife ________ clean the house on Tuesday?

________ , they ________ .

They ____________ clean the house on Wednesday.

9. ________ P.K. ________ stay in bed on Friday? ________ , he ________

10. ________ P.K. ________ play table tennis on Wednesday?

________ , he ________ . He ____________ play table tennis on Tuesday.

Exercise 6 *WWWWWH Questions: In the exercise below, the answer is given. Make the questions from the underlined part giving a hint to the "who", "what", "when", "where", "why" and "how" questions and should not be part of the answer.*

Ex. Who are you going to the party with?

I am going to go to the party with Marco.

1. ____ ?

She is going to go to Bali on her next vacation.

2. ____ ?

I am going to go to university on Friday because I am on the basketball team.

3. ____ ?

I am going to go to university on Friday to play basketball.

4. ____ ?

They are going to make dinner by watching YouTube videos.

5. ____ ?

He is going to study English with James.

6. ____ ?

They are going to play tennis on Saturday.

7. ____ ?

We are going to visit my aunt next week.

8. ____ ?

She is going to university by bus next week because her car is being fixed.

9. ____ ?

He is going to go to Busan for a party next weekend.

10. ____ ?

He is going to go to Busan for a party next weekend.

Phrasal Verbs using "LOOK":

Phrasal Verb	Meaning	Example
look after	a. to take care of something (돌보다.)	a. He looks after the children while his wife works all day.
look out	a. to yell when something dangerous is coming as a warning (조심하다.)	a. Look out! The ball is coming at us!
look into	a. to continue to get more information on something (조사하다.)	a. I need to look into getting a new credit card. This one has no benefits.
look great	a. to be beautiful in a set of clothing (멋지게 보이다.)	a. Wow. You look great in that dress! Where did you buy it?
look up	a. to search for information on (찾아보다.)	a. Hang on. I need to look up the definition of the word "gregarious".
look down on	a. to think worse of someone or something (무시하다.)	a. My mother looks down on people who don't have jobs but can work.
look ahead	a. to think about the future (미래를 바라보다.)	a. Look ahead to next year. All this work will be worth it.
look forward to	a. to be excited about something in the future (기대하다.)	a. I'm looking forward to my date this weekend. It should be great.

Exercise 7 *Match the phrasal verbs with the pictures.*

1.

2.

3.

4.

5.

6.

7.

8.

TOEIC VOCABULARY

Read the following common TOEIC words. Memorize so that you can do well on the TOEIC. Write the Korean and English in the space below two times to help you learn.

Cope with: 극복하다.
We have no system to cope with the avalanche that we have had this year.
올해 당한 눈사태를 극복할 수 있는 제도가 없다.

_________ / _________ _________ / _________

Correspondence: 통신, 교류.
We had been in correspondence with each other for many years before we met.
우리는 만나기 전 여러 해 동안 연락을 해 왔었다.

_________ / _________ _________ / _________

Costly: 비용이 드는.
Such a facility would be extremely costly to maintain.
이런 설비는 유지하는데 상당히 많은 비용이 들 수 있다.

_________ / _________ _________ / _________

Credit: 입금하다. 공로가 있다고 인정하다.
- The refund has been credited to your account.
환불금은 귀하의 계좌로 이미 입금처리 되었습니다.
- Edison is credited with inventing the light bulb.
Edison은 백열전구를 발명했다고 인정된다.
- The victory can be credited to the goal keeper.
이번 승리는 골 키퍼 덕택일 수 있다.

_________ / _________ _________ / _________

Critical: 비판적인, 매우 중요한.
Many analysts are critical of the result of the experiment.
많은 전문가들은 실험 결과에 대해 비판적이다.

_________ / _________ _________ / _________

Culminate: 최고조에 달하다.
A series of events for children will culminate in a speech contest.
아동을 위한 일련의 행사들은 웅변대회로 절정에 달할 것이다.

_________ / _________ _________ / _________

Cultivate: 기르다.
Try to cultivate a more positive attitude to life.
삶에 대해 좀 더 긍정적인 태도를 가져 보세요.

_________ / _________ _________ / _________

Customize: 주문에 맞추다.
Many companies try to customize their products according to the demand of the customers.
많은 기업들이 고객의 요구에 따라 제품을 주문에 맞추려고 애를 쓴다.

_________ / _________ _________ / _________

Defective: 결점이 있는.
This disease can be cured by eliminating defective genes in the marrow.
이 질병은 골수에 있는 결함유전자를 제거하면 치료할 수 있다.

_________ / _________ _________ / _________

Deficiency: 결함, 부족.
Some elderly people suffer from iron deficiency in their diet.
일부 노인들은 식사에 철분이 부족하여 고통을 겪는다.

_________ / _________ _________ / _________

Definitive: 결정적인.
The marketing team finally reached the definitive agreement to buy a start-up company.
마침내 마케팅 팀은 신생기업을 인수하기로 하는 최종 계약에 도달했다.

_________ / _________ _________ / _________

Demanding: 힘겨운, 요구사항이 많은.
Climbing is a physically demanding exercise.
등산은 육체적으로 힘겨운 운동이다.

_________ / _________ _________ / _________

Dependable: 의지할 수 있는.
For Israel, U.S.A. has been the most dependable ally.
이스라엘에게 미국은 가장 의지할 수 있는 동맹이다.

_________ / _________ _________ / _________

Deposit: 예치금, 보증금, 맡기다.
We will have to put down a deposit of 10 million Won on a house next month.
다음달에 집의 보증금 천만 원을 예치해야 할 것입니다.

_________ / _________ _________ / _________

Designate: 지정하다.
She has been designated to take over the position of marketing manager.
그녀가 마케팅 담당 과장직을 인수하도록 지정되었다.

__________ /__________ __________ /__________

Desirable: 바람직한.
The ability to speak a foreign language is highly desirable.
외국어를 구사할 수 있는 능력은 매우 바람직한 것이다.

__________ /__________ __________ /__________

Detail: 세부사항.
Full details of the plan will be announced.
계획의 전체 세부사항이 발표될 것입니다.

__________ /__________ __________ /__________

Deteriorate: 악화되다.
Their relationship deteriorated into the situation of slandering each other.
그들의 관계는 서로를 헐뜯는 상황으로 악화되었다.

__________ /__________ __________ /__________

Determine: 결정하다.
The volume of available funds determines the scale of a new project.
활용 가능한 자금의 규모가 새로운 사업의 규모를 결정한다.

__________ /__________ __________ /__________

Detour: 우회.
We should take a detour to avoid a traffic congestion.
교통 체증을 피하려면 우회로를 타야 한다.

__________ /__________ __________ /__________

Dismissal: 해고.
Several workers who had been fired sued the company for unfair dismissal.
해고된 몇몇 근로자들은 부당한 해고에 대해 회사를 고소했다.

__________ /__________ __________ /__________

Disposal: 제거, 처리, 처분.
The safe disposal of radioactive waste is a must for all of us.
방사능 폐기물을 안전하게 처리하는 것은 우리 모두에게 필수적인 것이다.
He has a lot of cash at his disposal.
그는 쓸 수 있는 현금이 많다.

__________ /__________ __________ /__________

Distract: 산만하게 하다.
Try not to distract the other students in class.
수업 중에 다른 학생들을 산만하지 않게 하도록 하세요.

__________ /__________ __________ /__________

Distribution: 유통, 분배.
The highly unequal distribution of wealth is the topic of today's conference.
상당히 불공평한 부의 분배가 오늘 회의의 주제입니다.

__________ /__________ __________ /__________

Diverse: 다양한.
Subjects as diverse as psychology and archaeology are covered in this book.
심리학과 고고학 같은 다양한 주제가 이 책에 나온다.

__________ /__________ __________ /__________

Donation: 기부.
I make a donation to a charity foundation every month.
나는 매달 자선단체에 기부하고 있습니다.

__________ /__________ __________ /__________

Durable: 지속 가능한, 견고한.
Wood is a durable and useful material.
목재는 견고하고 쓸모가 많은 재료이다.

__________ /__________ __________ /__________

Duration: 지속, 지속기간.
The courses of the universities in U.K. are of three years' duration.
영국의 대학 과정은 3년 간 지속된다.

__________ /__________ __________ /__________

Eager: 열심인.
I was eager to get back to work as soon as possible.
나는 가능한 조속히 업무에 복귀하고 싶었다.

__________ /__________ __________ /__________

Efficient: 실력 있는, 유능한.
Employers prefer efficient workers to talkative ones.
고용주들은 말 많은 직원보다 유능한 직원을 선호한다.

__________ /__________ __________ /__________

UNIT

9 This Is Fun, Isn't It?

Review Questions:

1. What is your favorite season? My favorite season is ______________________ .
2. What do you do in that season? In ______________ , I can ______________________ .
3. What do you want to be able to do in the future?

   In the future, I want to be able to ______________________________________ .

Warm-up Questions:

In Unit 8, we learned about how we can talk about the future. The future can be about our plans and what we will do, and the big things we want. These things are called our goals. The people in the picture are talking about their goals and dreams.

25. What are your goals?

    My main goal is to one day become a ______________________________ .
    (job you want)

26. What do you need to do to attain your goal?

Well, to become a ________________ , first I need to ________________________________ .
(job you want) (a step to do to get the job you want)

27. What will you do if you attain your dream?

If I can become a ________________ , the first thing I will do will be to ________________ .
(job you want) (thing you will do when you achieve dream)

Possible steps to achieving your goal:

– get a university degree
– get a good reference
– do well during internship
– take some special classes
– get some experience
– learn more about the job

ALTERNATIVE ANSWERS:

Not certain what you need to do:

– I don't know actually. I should do some more research.
– I am not certain what to do that would help me.
– ________________________________

Things you will do when you achieve dream

– save some money
– buy a nice house / car
– own my own business / become your own boss
– create better goals and try hard to achieve them
– take a long holiday / travel to some wonderful places
– get married and start a family
– ________________________________

Possible Goals:

– Hotelier
– ER Nurse
– Designer
– Architect
– Banker
– Company worker
– Musician
– Flight Attendant
– Actor
– Dental Hygienist

ALTERNATIVE ANSWERS:

If You Are Uncertain:

– I don't really have any solid goals right now.
– I'm not really sure. I've never thought about it.

Dialogue A: *"What are your goals?"*

Erica: Hey Michelle, 1. it's my turn to treat. What would you like to drink?

Michelle: I'd just love a café latte, with a bit of sugar. Thank you.

Erica: No problem.

Michelle: Hey Erica, what are your goals for the future?

Erica: Ha! I don't know? 2. Where is this coming from?

Michelle: Sorry. It's my business class. I have an assignment. I have to ask three of my closest friends about their goals. But mostly, it has me thinking about the future and my own plans.

Erica: Oh, ok. Well, I guess I want to run my own business one day. 3. Is that a good answer?

Michelle: Yeah, I guess so. But how will you do that? What kind of business will it be?

Erica: I'm not that sure. It's just something 4. I've always seen myself doing. I know I want to be the boss. Maybe in fashion. I don't like my job selling clothes, but I wouldn't mind owning the place and trying to make it more successful.

Michelle: Can't you be the boss in someone else's business? If someone else owns the place, you could still be the manager.

Erica: Yes, but I don't like the idea of making money for someone else. How about you, Michelle? Any plans for the future?

Michelle: Just between us, 5. I have no idea whatsoever, but don't tell anyone. Most business major students seem to have this very detailed plan.

Erica: Don't worry. Your secret's safe with me.

Substitution Drill: Use the following responses in the above conversation.

		A. FORMAL	B. INFORMAL
1.	it's my turn to treat.	It's my turn to buy. You bought last time.	I think you got the last one so this is on me.
2.	Where is this coming from?	What is the reason you are asking this?	Where did this topic come from?
3.	Is that a good answer?	Is that the kind of information you want?	Is that what you are looking for?
4.	I've always seen myself doing.	I've thought my future holds.	I've always dreamed about.
5.	I have no idea whatsoever.	I don't have any ideas.	I don't have any clue.

Grammar Gallery 1: *Tag Questions Part 1*

Pronoun	Affirmative	Negative(not)	Yes/No Question(?)	Tag Question
I	I am	I am not (I'm not)	Am I...?	I am..., aren't I? I am not..., am I?
You We They	You are We are They are	You are not (You aren't) We are not (We aren't) They are not (They aren't)	Are you...? Are we...? Are they...?	You are..., aren't you? You aren't..., are you?
He She It	He is She is It is	He is not (He isn't) She is not (She isn't) It is not (It isn't)	Is he...? Is she...?	He is..., isn't he? He isn't..., is he?

Tag questions:
Tag questions are used most often when you think you know the answer and want confirmation. This kind of question can be tricky to make and answer, but also can be very helpful when we need to get an answer quickly. With tag questions we are able to reduce all questions down to a "yes" or "no" answer. You're beginning to understand, aren't you?
(부가의문문 : 부가의문문은 말하는 사람이 답을 알고 있다고 생각하지만 확인을 하고자 할 때 빈번히 사용됩니다. 이런 종류의 질문은 하기도 어렵고 답하기도 어렵지만 답을 빨리 듣고자 할 때 요긴합니다. 부가의문문을 활용하면 모든 질문에 대한 답을 "예" 또는 "아니오"라는 답으로 유도할 수 있습니다. 이제 이해가 가시죠?)

NOTE: A positive sentence always uses a negative question tag and a negative sentence always uses a positive question tag.
(긍정문은 항상 부정 부가의문문을 사용하고 부정문은 항상 긍정 부가의문문을 사용합니다.)

negative sentence	→	positive question tag
He is not Korean,		is he?

positive sentence	→	negative question tag
He is Korean,		isn't he?

Exercise 1 *Write the opposite sentence (negative sentence or the positive sentence) for the following. Notice, they are all using "to be" verb. Use the contraction form (isn't / aren't).*

Ex. He is good at English. He isn't good at English.

1. You are tall. ______________________ .
2. She isn't happy. ______________________ .
3. They are angry. ______________________ .
4. You aren't real. ______________________ .
5. It is big. ______________________ .
6. This is scary. ______________________ .
7. There are four oranges. ______________________ .
8. You are not serious. ______________________ .
9. This isn't really happening. ______________________ .
10. We are going home. ______________________ .
11. He isn't Canadian. ______________________ .
12. I am not sleepy. ______________________ .

RULES: To make a tag question: 부가의문문 만드는 순서:

1. Change "." to ","
   "마침표"를 "쉼표"로 바꾸세요.
2. Find the "to be" verb (am, is , are), and write it one more time.
   "be" 동사(am, is, are)를 찾아서 한 번 더 쓰세요.
3. If there is no "not", add a "not" to the verb. (is ➡ isn't, are ➡ aren't)
   "not"이 없으면 동사에 "not"을 첨가하세요. If there is a "not", take it out. (isn' t → is, aren' t → are) "not"이 있으면 제거하세요.
4. Write the pronoun again (I, you , we, they, he , she , it) and "?".
   대명사(I, you, we, they, he, she, it)를 다시 사용하고 "물음표"를 붙이세요.

Ex. She is tall.		Ex. She isn't tall.	
1. change "." to ","	➡ She is tall,	1. change "." to ","	➡ She isn't tall,
2. verb " is"	➡ She is tall, **is**	2. verb " isn't"	➡ She isn't tall, **isn't**
3. add "not"	➡ She is tall, is**n't**	3. take out "not"	➡ She isn't tall, is~~n't~~
4. write pronoun +"?"	➡ She is tall, isn't **she?**	4. write pronoun +"?"	➡ She isn't tall, is **she?**

Exercise 2 *Circle the correct tag question ending.*

Ex. She is beautiful,	is she?	isn't she?
1. The cat is scary,	isn't it?	isn't they?
2. He isn't tall,	is he?	isn't he?
3. They are listening,	isn't they?	aren't they?
4. The computers are broken,	isn't it?	aren't they?
5. The students aren't here,	are they?	aren't they?
6. The computer is broken,	isn't it?	aren't they?
7. She is the new boss,	is she?	isn't she?
8. Susan and Jill aren't friendly,	is they?	are they?
9. You are a student,	are you?	aren't you?
10. The food is great,	is it?	isn't it?

Exercise 3 *Matching: Find the correct tag question for each of the following statements.*

1. The bird is flying in the sky,	A) aren't we?
2. I am late,	B) are they?
3. They aren't here yet,	C) aren't I?
4. We are tired today,	D) aren't they?
5. Bill and Susan are dating,	E) isn't she?
6. Jill is thirsty,	F) isn't it?

SPECIAL RULE: I am... aren't I?

(특수한 규칙 : I am일 때의 부가의문문은 aren't I?)

Exercise 4 *Complete the sentences with the correct tag question.*

1. We aren't late, ____________? Yes, we are.
2. He isn't mad, ____________? No, he isn't.
3. You are trying to pass, ____________? Yes, I am.

4. She is a good dancer, ______________? No, she isn't.
5. The movie isn't great, ______________? No, it isn't.
6. They aren't in class, ______________? Yes, they are.
7. We are great, ______________? No, we are not.
8. It isn't open, ______________? Yes, it is.
9. She isn't very friendly, ______________? No, she isn't.
10. You aren't playing a cell phone game, ______________? Yes, you are.

Impossible answers: (다음과 같은 답변은 불가능합니다.)

Yes, it isn't. ✘ No, it is. ✘

Yes, they aren't. ✘ No, they are. ✘

Yes,............ not ??? ✘

No,............... not ??? ✘

These often confuse speakers more than confirm truth, so avoid these.
(이런 표현은 화자에게 확인이 아니라 오히려 혼란스럽게 하니 피하셔야 합니다.)

Conversation Corner: *How to answer a tag question.*

The answer is always a reflection of the truth.
부가의문문에 답하는 요령. (답은 항상 사실의 확인이어야 합니다.)

Ex. Snow is white, isn't it? **Yes, it is.**
Snow isn't white, is it? **Yes, it is.**
(Snow = white: TRUE: yes!)
(질문 내용의 긍정 부정에 관계 없이 눈의 색은 흰색입니다. 그러니까 "네, 흰색입니다." "아니, 흰색입니다." 모두 "Yes, it is." 라고 표현해야 합니다.)

- Birds are animals that fly, aren't they? **Yes, they are.**
  (새는 날 수 있는 동물입니다, 그렇지 않습니까? 네, 날 수 있는 동물입니다.)
  (Bird = flying animals: True: Yes!) (새 = 날 수 있는 동물: 진실이니 "Yes!" 라고 답합니다.)
- Birds aren't animals that fly, are they? **Yes, they are.**
  (새는 날 수 있는 동물이 아닙니다, 그렇습니까? 아니오, 날 수 있는 동물입니다.)
- The computers aren't broken, are they? (컴퓨터 고장나지 않았지요, 그렇죠?)
  ➡ **Yes, they are** (= yes, the computers are broken) (아니오, 고장났습니다.)
  ➡ **No, they aren't** (= no, the computers are NOT broken) (네, 고장나지 않았습니다.)

Exercise 5 *Answer the following tag questions. Then write the meaning.*

Ex. He is handsome, isn't he? No, he isn't. (He isn't handsome.)

1. The monkey is scary, isn't it? Yes, ____________ . (____________ .)
2. The boys are tired, aren't they? No, ____________ . (____________ .)
3. The class isn't dirty, is it? Yes, ____________ . (____________ .)
4. The teacher is fun, isn't he? No, ____________ . (____________ .)
5. Bananas are yellow, aren't they? Yes, ____________ . (____________ .)

(Now you think about the "yes" or "no" answer. Compare with a partner)

(이제 "Yes" 또는 "No"라는 답변에 대해 생각해 보세요. 파트너와 비교해 보세요.)

6. Winter isn't cold in Korea, is it? ____________ . (____________ .)
7. Bruce Willis is a famous actor, isn't he? ____________ . (____________ .)
8. Jeju is a beautiful island, isn't it? ____________ . (____________ .)
9. University classes aren't boring, are they? ____________ . (____________ .)
10. The weather is nice today, isn't it? ____________ . (____________ .)

Exercise 6 *Double exercise: Make the tag question then answer the questions. (* two answers possible)*

1. They aren't quiet, ____________ ? No, ____________ .
2. The students are excellent, ____________ ? Yes, ____________ .
3. The lady is watching us, ____________ ? Yes, ____________ .
4. You are working in a group, ____________ ?

   No, I ____________ .* No, we ____________ .
5. Bob is a nice guy, ____________ ? Yes, ____________ .
6. Sharon isn't very nice, ____________ ? No, ____________ .
7. I am nervous, ____________ ?

   No, ____________ . * No, ____________ .
8. Dogs are too friendly, ____________ ? Yes, ____________ .
9. The classrooms are too hot, ____________ ? No, ____________ .
10. Chris is a quiet person, ____________ ? Yes, ____________ .

Exercise 7 *Putting it all together.*

These kinds of tag question rules apply to all verbs that can take "not".

is / isn't are / aren't was / wasn't were / weren't can / can't
will / won't would / wouldn't could / couldn't

1. They are all dancing, ____________________ ?
2. Julian can't play chess, ____________________ ?
3. Patrick is athletic, ____________________ ?
4. You aren't afraid of foreigners, ____________________ ?
5. He won't eat his vegetables, ____________________ ?
6. Michelle isn't at home, ____________________ ?
7. Bill is wearing glasses, ____________________ ?
8. I'm too short, ____________________ ?
9. Bethany is late again, ____________________ ?
10. Alan will bring his umbrella, ____________________ ?
11. You're very lucky, ____________________ ?
12. She is from South Africa, ____________________ ?
13. You were from Chicago, ____________________ ?
14. Donald is living in Toronto, ____________________ ?
15. Your brother was in Jamaica, ____________________ ?
16. You would say that, ____________________ ?
17. I am very tall, ____________________ ?

Dialogue B: *"P.K. or Olly?"*

Erica: Hi Michelle, 1. how are things?
Michelle: Yeah, good! What's up?
Erica: I'm just looking for Olly. You haven't seen him, have you?
Michelle: 2. Sorry, who?
Erica: Oh, P.K., a bunch of us started calling him Olly. He says he doesn't like being called P.K.
Michelle: Really? OK, I didn't know that. I always call him P.K.
Erica: So, you haven't seen him then, have you?
Michelle: No, he's not hiding around here anywhere.
Erica: Alright, 3. I've got a million things to do. I'll see you later.
Michelle: OK then, bye.

Michelle: Hi P.K., I've been meaning to ask you something.
P.K.: Oh yeah, what's that?
Michelle: You don't like being called P.K., do you?
P.K.: Why? Who told you that?
Michelle: Is it true?
P.K.: Erica told you, didn't she?
Michelle: 4. Never mind who told me. Should I call you Olly instead?
P.K.: It's not a big deal. It's just that my friends from high school call me Olly. 5. I don't really care, to be honest.
Michelle: OK, Olly. Whatever you say, Olly. See you later, Olly.
P.K.: Yeah, yeah. Very funny.

Substitution Drill: Use the following responses in the above conversation.

		A. FORMAL	B. INFORMAL
1.	how are things?	how are things going?	are things going OK?
2.	Sorry, who?	Who is Olly?	I don't know an "Olly". Who is that?
3.	I've got a million things to do.	I'm very busy today.	I have a lot of stuff to do today.
4.	Never mind who told me.	Who said it isn't important.	It doesn't matter who said that.
5.	I don't really care, to be honest.	It doesn't matter to me either way.	I don't mind either, if I have to be honest.

Dialogue Cont'd:

Erica: Hey Olly, wait up!

P.K.: Oh, hey Erica, what's up?

Erica: I've been looking for you everywhere. Are we still going rock climbing later on?

P.K.: Yeah, for sure. I've been looking forward to it. I haven't been climbing in ages.

Erica: Cool. I have to grab a few things from home first. Can you give me a lift?

P.K.: Sure, but listen. I want you to stop telling people to call me Olly, OK?

Erica: Sorry. I didn't know it was a secret.

P.K.: It's not. I just don't want everyone knowing about my life. You understand, don't you?

Erica: Yeah OK... Mr. Mysterious, let's get out of here.

Grammar Gallery 2: *Tag Questions Part 2*

Earlier in this unit, tag questions with verbs that easily add "not" were discussed. These verbs were:

is / isn't are / aren't was / wasn't were / weren't can / can't will / won't
would / wouldn't could / couldn't have / haven't has / hasn't

These are easy because they readily take the "not" verb into a contraction. But other verbs are not so simple.
(위 동사들은 "not"을 쉽게 축약할 수 있어서 쉽습니다. 하지만 다른 동사들은 그렇게 단순하지 않습니다.)

For example, look at the opposites of the normal verbs and how they are used below.
(예를 들어 다음에 나오는 일반 동사의 부정형을 보고 어떻게 사용되는가 살펴보세요.)

- He plays soccer. He doesn't play soccer.
- We went to the store. We didn't go to the store.
- I eat kimchi. I don't eat kimchi.

This affects the tag question as well, when we need the opposite, as seen below:
(아래에 예시된 것처럼 이런 점이 반대 진술을 해야 하는 부가의문문에도 영향을 줍니다.)

- He plays soccer, **doesn't he?**
- We went to the store, **didn't he?**
- I eat kimchi, **don't I?**

Another Special Rule: (또 하나의 특수 규칙)

- Let's... , shall we?

Ex. Let's go swimming, shall we?

Exercise 8 *Complete these tag questions that are past simple or present simple.*

1. She was your friend, ______________?
2. Olly eats lamb, ______________?
3. You speak Korean, ______________?
4. Michelle doesn't dance, ______________?
5. Will didn't play basketball, ______________?
6. Children like cartoons, ______________?
7. You understand this, ______________?
8. You drove to Busan last year, ______________?
9. Erica was with you yesterday, ______________?
10. You did your homework, ______________?
11. It rained yesterday, ______________?
12. I don't like squid, ______________?
13. He doesn't run, ______________?
14. You practice the piano, ______________?
15. You didn't run here, ______________?
16. These questions were easy, ______________?

Phrasal Verbs using "TRY", "BREAK" and "RUN":

Phrasal Verb	Meaning	Example
Try on	a. To wear something to check if it is the right size (옷이 몸에 맞는지 입어보다.)	a. He agreed to try the hat on.
Try out	a. To test something (시험하다)	a. We tried the headphones out before we bought them.
Break down	a. To get upset or to malfunction (우울해지다, 고장나다.)	a. The car always breaks down. The woman broke down crying.
Break up	a. To end a relationship (관계를 정리하다.)	a. She decided she and her boyfriend had to break up.

Break out	**a.** To escape or to suddenly get a skin blemish (탈출하다, 또는 갑자기 피부에 상처를 입다.)	**a.** He broke out of prison. Her skin broke out in a rash.
Break in	**a.** To illegally access a property (침입하다.)	**a.** Someone broke in last night. They took the T.V.!
Run out	**a.** To exhaust a supply (부족하다.)	**a.** We've run out of toilet paper.
Run over	**a.** To hit someone with a car (차량으로 치다.)	**a.** My sister ran over a cat once.
Run into	**a.** To meet someone accidentally (우연히 만나다.)	**a.** We might run into each other at Lotte World one day.
Run away	**a.** To leave suddenly, driven by emotion (감정이 상해서 갑자기 떠나다.)	**a.** Peter Pan decided to run away from the orphanage.

After reading and repeating these sentences, try to make one more example sentence of your own for your four favorite phrasal verbs. You can use the table below to record your phrasal verbs and new example sentences.
(위 문장을 읽고 반복한 뒤 자신이 좋아하는 구동사 4개를 활용하여 스스로 예문을 만들어 보세요. 구동사와 새로운 예문을 아래 도표에 써 보세요.)

PHRASAL VERBS	NEW EXAMPLE SENTENCES

TOEIC VOCABULARY

Read the following common TOEIC words. Memorize so that you can do well on the TOEIC. Write the Korean and English in the space below two times to help you learn.

Cautious: 조심스러운.
The air-pollution prevention bureau has reacted with cautious optimism to the warning.
대기오염 방지국은 이번 경고에 대해 조심스러운 낙관론으로 반응했다.

__________ / __________ __________ / __________

Certificate: 증명서, 수료증.
Applicants should enclose a degree certificate with an application form.
지원자들은 지원서와 함께 학위 증명서를 동봉해야 한다.

__________ / __________ __________ / __________

Clerical: 업무상의.
Don't think much of the matter which is nothing but a clerical error.
업무상 실수에 불과한 사안을 너무 깊게 생각하지 마세요.

__________ / __________ __________ / __________

Collaboration: 협업.
The project has involved a close collaboration with the geology department.
이번 사업은 지질학과의 긴밀한 협업이 포함되어 있다.

__________ / __________ __________ / __________

Colleague: 동료.
He discussed the matter with some of his colleagues.
그는 동료 몇 명과 그 문제를 상의했다.

__________ / __________ __________ / __________

Commit: 헌신하다.
I'd committed myself and there was no turning back.
나는 최선을 다했었고 따라서 돌이킬 수가 없었다.

__________ / __________ __________ / __________

Compensation: 보상.
I haven't received any compensation from the company for the damage caused to my property.
나의 재산상 피해에 대해 회사로부터 어떤 보상도 받지 못했다.

__________ / __________ __________ / __________

Complaint: 불만.
Sales people are trained to deal with customer complaints in a friendly manner.
판매 사원들은 고객의 불만사항을 친근하게 처리하도록 교육받는다.

__________ / __________ __________ / __________

Compliance: 준수, 순응.
The staff involved are being monitored to ensure compliance with the policy.
관련 직원들은 본 정책 준수를 확실하게 하기 위해 감시되고 있다.

__________ / __________ __________ / __________

Complimentary: 무료의.
There are two complimentary bottles of mineral water in the hotel room.
호텔 객실에는 생수 두 병이 무료로 제공된다.

__________ / __________ __________ / __________

Comply with: 준수하다.
Any failure to comply with the regulations may result in prosecution.
규정을 준수하지 않으면 기소될 수도 있습니다.

__________ / __________ __________ / __________

Comprehensive: 포괄적인.
The following instruction does not aim to be totally comprehensive.
다음 안내사항은 완전하게 포괄적이지는 않습니다.

__________ / __________ __________ / __________

Compromise: 타협하다.
If you compromise your principles, you are almost lost.
당신의 원칙과 타협하려 한다면 당신은 거의 패배한 것이나 다름없다.

__________ / __________ __________ / __________

Concentrate: 집중하다.
Assembly of the airplane is concentrated in San Francisco.
비행기 조립은 San Francisco에 집중되어 있다.

__________ / __________ __________ / __________

Concerning: ~에 관하여.
The police station has received a lot of calls from

many people concerning missing parents.
경찰서는 실종된 부모들에 관해 많은 사람들로부터 많은 전화를 받았다.

_____ / _____ _____ / _____

Confidential: 비밀의.
Doctors and nurses are required to keep patients' records completely confidential.
의사와 간호사는 환자의 기록을 철저하게 비밀에 부쳐야 한다.

_____ / _____ _____ / _____

Congratulate: 축하하다.
People congratulated me on my success in business.
사람들이 나의 사업상 성공을 축하해 주었다.

_____ / _____ _____ / _____

Consecutive: 연속적인.
Can he win the title for the third consecutive year?
그가 3년째 연속으로 그 직위를 차지할 수 있을까?
It has been raining for five consecutive days.
5일 계속해서 비가 오고 있네요.

_____ / _____ _____ / _____

Consent: 동의, 동의하다.
At last, her parents gave their consent to the marriage.
마침내 그녀의 부모는 이 결혼에 동의해 주었다.
A patient can refuse consent for a particular treatment at any time.
환자는 어느 때라도 특정 치료법에 대해 동의를 거부할 수 있다.
Most celebrities are happy to have their names used for publicity if this is done with their prior consent.
대부분의 유명인사들은 사전 동의만 거친다면 자신의 이름이 홍보 목적으로 기꺼이 사용되도록 할 것이다.

_____ / _____ _____ / _____

Considerable: 상당한.
The rumor has aroused considerable doubt about his ability.
이번 소문이 그의 능력에 관한 상당한 의혹을 불러일으켰다.

_____ / _____ _____ / _____

Consistent: 한결 같은.
Your speech and behavior should be consistent in all aspects.
당신의 말과 행동은 모든 면에서 일관성이 있어야 합니다.

_____ / _____ _____ / _____

Constant: 지속적인.
He kept in constant contact with his family while he was abroad.
그는 해외에 체류하는 동안 가족과 지속적인 연락을 취했다.

_____ / _____ _____ / _____

Constructive: 건설적인.
We welcome any constructive criticism.
어떤 건설적인 비판도 환영한다.

_____ / _____ _____ / _____

Consult: 자문을 구하다, 진찰을 받다.
As soon as symptoms appear, consult a doctor without delay.
증세가 나타나는 즉시 지체하지 말고 의사를 찾아가세요.

_____ / _____ _____ / _____

Consumption: 소비.
The consumption of alcohol on the premises is forbidden.
구역 내에서는 술을 마실 수 없습니다.

_____ / _____ _____ / _____

Contingent: 의지하는, 우발적인.
Further investment is contingent upon the long-term development plan.
추가 투자는 장기 개발계획에 달려 있다.

_____ / _____ _____ / _____

Contradict: 모순되다.
The two statements of the accused contradict each other.
피고의 두 진술은 서로 앞뒤가 맞지 않는다.

_____ / _____ _____ / _____

Contribute: 공헌하다, 기부하다.
Civil servants must not contribute to political campaigns in any case.
공무원들은 어떤 경우라도 정치 행사에 공헌해서는 안 된다.

_____ / _____ _____ / _____

Contribution: 기여, 공헌, 기부.
Have you been making regular contributions to a pension plan?
연금에 정기적으로 납부금을 내고 있습니까?

_____ / _____ _____ / _____

Convene: 소집하다.
The chairman of the board convened an emergency meeting to discuss the pending matter.
이사회장은 당면 문제를 상의하기 위해 긴급 회의를 소집했다.

_____ / _____ _____ / _____

UNIT 10 Vacation Is Around the Corner!

Review Questions:

1. What are your goals?

   My main goal is to one day become a

   ______________________ .
   (job you want)

2. What do you need to do to attain your goal?

   Well, to become a ______________________ ,
   (job you want)

   first I need to ______________________ .
   (a step to do to get the job you want)

3. What are you bad at? What are your weaknesses?

   I'm bad at (My weaknesses are) ______________________ .
   (activity)

Warm-up Questions:

28. Why do you study English?

    I study English because I think ______________________ .

29. How can speaking English be helpful in your future?

    In the future, English can help me when (if) ______________________ .

30. How can you continue to study English on your own?

    To continue my English study, I can ______________________ .

Brainstorming:

How speaking English can be helpful in your future	How to study English on your own
– help me when travelling abroad – help me when trying to get a job – –	– listen to English radio – study English on my cell phone with language apps –

Dialogue A: *"I need a part time job!"*

Wei: 1. Any luck with the job hunting?

Erica: Not really, I'm still thinking about what I really want to do. How about you?

Wei: Almost. I have an interview at the library tomorrow evening. I love reading, so I'm hoping 2. it will work out. I hate applying for jobs though, it's so stressful. If it doesn't work, I can always work for Biju at the Indian restaurant.

Erica: Well that sounds fun too! Wouldn't you like working there?

Wei: It's hard work. I don't dislike being a server, but I really hate doing dishes. And every evening, I need to wash my clothes because of the smell. It gets so noisy too… 3. Honestly, I really prefer being in a library.

Erica: Well, at least it's an option… I don't know where to start looking. I don't mind working hard, and I like being around many people. I 4. can't stand sitting down for too long, especially staring at a computer screen. Do you have any suggestions?

Wei: That's funny, we are so different. But wait… you like working hard, being around people… Hey, you should work at the Indian restaurant! At least until you decide what you want to do for the future. I'm sure Biju would love you.

Erica: Oh… that's a great idea! When can I interview?

Wei: Oh come on! I'll 5. put in a good word for you, I'm sure you don't have to interview… if you promise to work hard!

Erica: Great! I need to practice my cooking skills!

Wei: Huh… Erica, I think you will be mostly doing dishes…

Substitution Drill: Use the following responses in the above conversation.

		A. FORMAL	B. INFORMAL
1.	Any luck with the job hunting?	How has the search for a new job been going?	Did you manage to find a nice job?
2.	it will work out.	it will go well and I get the job.	my interview will get me the job.
3.	Honestly, I really prefer being in a library.	If I'm truthful, I would like the library job more.	Honestly, I am hoping for the library job.
4.	can't stand sitting down for too long,	really don't like sitting in a chair for a long time,	don't ever want to have to sit for a long time,
5.	put in a good word for you,	tell them about your good qualities,	tell them about you,

Conversation Corner: *Politely giving and asking for advice*

Making requests, or asking for help, can be done in many ways. As always, when asking someone else for a favor or giving advice there are many things you might be worried about. When asking for help, you do not want the other person to feel like they cannot refuse, or that you think they are not busy. If you are giving advice, you do not want the person to be offended, to feel like you are judging them, etc.

(요청하거나 도와달라고 부탁하는 것은 여러 가지로 가능합니다. 항상 그렇듯이 누군가에게 부탁을 한다거나 충고를 할 때에는 신경을 써야 할 것이 많이 있습니다. 도와달라고 할 때 상대방이 거절할 수 없다는 느낌을 받는 것을 당신은 원치 않을 것이고, 상대방이 한가하다고 당신이 생각하지 않기를 원합니다. 당신이 충고를 한다면 당신은 상대방이 기분이 상하는 것을 원치 않을 것이고 당신이 상대방을 평가하고 있다는 느낌을 받고 싶지 않을 것입니다.)

Here are a few hints that you can keep in mind in such situations.

(이런 상황에서 기억해야 할 몇 가지 힌트가 있습니다.)

1. Choose appropriate verbs:

When using modal verbs, understand the difference between the "softer" verbs such as ***could, may, might,*** and ***would*** which sound more respectful, and the "harder" ones such as ***can, ought to, should, must, will*** which sound much more direct.

(조동사를 사용할 때에는 존중의 의미를 지닌 것으로 들리는 could, may, might, would과 같은 "부드러운 뉘앙스"의 조동사와 한결 더 직접적으로 들리는 can, ought to, should, must, will 같은 "강한 뉘앙스"의 조동사의 차이를 이해해야 합니다.)

Look at the following sentences and notice which ones sound "softer" or "harder".

a) – *Can* you close the window? – *Could* you close the window

b) – *Can* I see your ID? – *May* I see your ID

c) – You *ought to* talk to her. – You *might* want to talk to her

2. The longer the better.

Have you noticed how using longer sentences to ask for something usually sounds less direct, and therefore more polite? Notice how the modal verbs help being even more polite (뭔가를 요청할 때 좀 더 긴 문장을 사용하는 것이 좀 더 부드럽고 그 결과 더 정중하게 들리는 것을 눈치채셨습니까? 조동사를 사용하면 더욱 더 정중하게 보일 수 있다는 것을 주의하세요.)

- *Can you show me…*
- *Would you mind showing me…*
- *Would it be possible to show me…*
- *Do you think it might be possible to show me…*

NOTE: The usage of "please".

"please" makes the sentence more polite. But alone, it may not be enough. Choose your vocabulary well. ("please"의 활용. "please"를 사용하면 문장이 더 정중하게 들립니다. 하지만 홀로 쓰면 충분하지 않습니다. 어휘를 잘 선택하세요.)

Ex. Shut up, please! (not polite)
Would you be quiet, please? (polite)

3. Use "please" ... or not?

We have all been told that using "please" always makes a sentence sound more polite. Look at the following sentences; do you agree? Does it always sound better with "please"? ("please"를 사용하면 문장이 더 정중하게 들릴 수 있다는 것을 알았습니다. 다음 문장을 보세요, 동의하십니까? "please"를 사용하니까 늘 더 좋게 들리시나요?)

- Take off you shoes.
- Take off your shoes, please.
- Would it be possible to turn the volume down?
- Would it be possible to turn the volume down, please?

Practice with a partner:

ASKING:	
1. to borrow their book	**2.** to help you study English
3. to help them with the homework	**4.** to move their chair over a bit
5. to help you understand the teacher	**6.** to sing a song for you

Grammar Gallery 1: *Verbs + gerunds / verbs + Infinitives:*

1. Some verbs are always followed by *gerunds.*

Verbs + gerunds	
• Recommend • Enjoy • Dislike • Suggest • Mind	• They recommend **staying** home. • He enjoys **snowboarding.** • They dislike **shopping.** • We suggest **trying** kimchi. • I don't mind **staying** home.

Gerunds look and sound like the *~ing* form of verbs used in the present continuous tense but function differently. They are sometimes called "noun verbs" because they make verbs act like nouns. Their meaning is "the act of doing that verb."

(동명사는 현재진행시제에서 사용하는 동사의 "ing" 형태와 같아 보이고 음도 같습니다. 이들이 "동사-명사"로 불리는 이유는 동사를 명사처럼 사용되게 하기 때문입니다. 그 의미는 "해당 동사의 행위"입니다.)

Because gerunds look like the *~ing* form of a verb, it is easy to confuse both. You can tell that a word is a gerund if you can replace it with another noun:

(동명사가 동사의 "~ing" 형태와 같아 보이기 때문에 두 가지를 혼동하기 쉽습니다. 다른 명사로 바꾸어 쓸 수 있으면 그 단어는 동명사라고 할 수 있습니다.)

• I like shopping. ➡ I like *ice cream.* ✔
(The sentence is still grammatically correct: shopping is a gerund)
(이 문장은 문법적으로 옳습니다. shopping이 동명사입니다.)

• I am shopping. ➡ I am *ice cream.* ✘
(The sentence makes no sense: in this case, shopping is an ~ing verb)
(이 문장은 의미가 통하지 않습니다. 이 경우 shopping은 동사에 "~ing"를 첨가한 것입니다.)

2. Other verbs are always followed by *infinitives.*

Verbs + infinitives	
• Need	• I need **to study.**
• Want	• He wants **to go.**
• Promise	• I promise **to call** you.
• Hope	• We hope **to get** an autograph.
• Plan	• They plan **to visit** Thailand.

There is no clear rule as to which verbs must be followed by gerunds, and which ones should be followed by infinitives.
(어떤 동사 뒤에는 동명사가 와야 하고 어떤 동사 뒤에는 부정사가 와야 하는가에 대한 분명한 규칙은 없습니다.)

3. A few verbs can be followed by *gerunds or infinitives.*

Verbs + infinitives or gerunds		
• Like	• I like **studying.**	= I like **to study.**
• Love	• I love **shopping.**	= I love **to shop.**
• Hate	• I hate **driving.**	= I hate **to drive.**
• Prefer	• I prefer **biking.**	= I prefer **to bike.**
• Start	• I started **painting.**	= I started **to paint.**

For these verbs, the meaning of the sentence remains the same whether they are followed by a gerund or infinitive.
(위 동사들의 경우 동명사나 부정사 어느 것이 와도 문장의 의미는 동일합니다.)

Exercise 1 *Fill in the blanks with the "gerund" form of the given verb.*

1. I enjoy ______________ (study).
2. She dislikes ______________ (read).
3. We don't mind ______________ (wait).
4. He suggested ______________ (try) the pasta.
5. I recommend ______________ (bring) extra clothes.
6. Do you mind ______________ (say) it once more?
7. I want to start ______________ (play) the piano.
8. He prefers ______________ (go) home by bus.
9. Do you like ______________ (dance)?
10. I loved ______________ (receive) your letter.
11. I finished ______________ (do) my homework.
12. Can you imagine ______________ (live) here?

Exercise 2 *Fill in the blanks with the "infinitive" form of the given verb.*

1. We need ______________ (take) a break .
2. We plan ______________ (arrive) by 4 p.m.
3. She hopes ______________ (get) a good grade.
4. You promised ______________ (call) me back!
5. He wants ______________ (see) a movie.
6. Lisa likes ______________ (party) on the weekend.
7. Has he started ______________ (look) at new houses?
8. I hate ______________ (eat) dinner alone.

9. I prefer ________ (drink) water.

10. We love ________ (go) fishing.

11. I agree ________ (help) you.

12. We decided ________ (stay) home.

Exercise 3 *Fill in the blanks with either the "gerund" or "infinitive" form of the given verb.*

1. Would you mind ________ (turn) the volume?

2. We need ________ (go) shopping.

3. Can we start ________ (write) now?

4. I recommend ________ (see) that movie.

5. Do you plan ________ (visit) your family?

6. Maybe he likes ________ (be) alone.

7. I suggest ________ (meet) at 8 p.m.?

8. I really want ________ (eat) ramyeon.

9. James prefers ________ (get up) early.

10. I promise not ________ (be) late.

11. I don't dislike ________ (snowboard) , but I prefer ________ (ski).

Exercise 4 *Sometimes, both a gerund or an infinitive is acceptable. For each picture, write two sentences: one using a verb + gerund, one using a verb + infinitive.*

1. A) He *enjoys* **reading** books.

   B) He *likes* **to read**.

2. A) ______________________________.

   B) ______________________________.

3. A) ______________________________.

   B) ______________________________.

4. A) ______________________________.

   B) ______________________________.

5. A) ______________________________.

   B) ______________________________.

Exercise 5 *The dating game. Read the descriptions and fill in the blanks.*

(청취연습 : 데이트 게임. 설명을 잘 읽고 빈 칸을 채우세요.)

HI, I'm Mike, 32, a typical California outdoor guy. I love anything as long as it is outside. Camping, hiking, surfing, you name it. But keep me indoors for too long and who knows what will happen.

Name: ______________________

Likes: ______________________

Doesn't like: ______________________

Hi, my name is Liz and I'm into art. I love everything related to painting and sculpture. I always wanted to be an artist myself, but I guess I'm just better at looking than making. I'm not very athletic and I hate running, but I'm happy to go for a long walk.

Name: ______________________

Likes: ______________________

Doesn't like: ______________________

Hello, my name is Brent and I'm 42 years old. I work for the National Astronomy Center in Boston. I spend most of the time here, in this lab during the week, but on the weekends, I'm open to anything... well, anything that doesn't involve sports. I'm not too much of a sports guy, but I do enjoy traveling.

Name: ______________________

Likes: ______________________

Doesn't like: ______________________

Hi, I'm Lisa, and... this is my horse Deby. We are together most of the time, but I promise to share! My father raised horses, and so I spent most of my life outside, on the ranch. I live in the city now, and work in advertising. But I get out as much as I can. If I'm not in my office, you know where to find me!

Name: ______________________

Likes: ______________________

Doesn't like: ______________________

Exercise 6 *Now choose which people are best matches and say why.*

- I think ______________ and ______________ are a good match because ______________

____.

- ____.

____.

Exercise 7 *Write your own dating description: Say your name and at least 3 things you like and 3 things you dislike. Then read your description to a partner and listen to your partner's answer. Write down your partner's answers. Then talk with a new partner. What do you have in common?*

(데이트 상대에 대해 기술해 보세요. 자신의 이름을 말하고 좋아하는 점 최소한 3가지와 싫어하는 점 최소한 3가지를 말해 보세요. 그리고 나서 파트너에게 읽어주고 파트너가 좋아하고 싫어하는 점을 들어 보세요. 파트너가 말한 내용을 기록하세요. 다른 파트너와 대화를 하세요. 공통점을 발견했나요?)

YOUR ANSWERS	
Likes:	1. ______________
	2. ______________
	3. ______________
Dislikes:	1. ______________
	2. ______________
	3. ______________

Dialogue B: *"Do you have any plans for the break?"*

Erica: Only a week left! I feel like I'm already on vacation!

Michelle: I know. I can't believe we are almost done! Did you book your flights to Hanoi yet?

Erica: Yes, 1. we booked the flights. We plan to leave next Saturday, but we are still hesitating about the hotel. You were in Vietnam last year, weren't you? 2. Do you have any suggestions?

Michelle: Hmm, let me think... maybe you should look for reviews online, or how about contacting some youth hostels? They are usually very friendly, and quite cheap.

Erica: That's a good idea. 3. I hadn't thought about that. How about you, Marco? Did you find your part-time job?

Marco: Oh, I'm not really thinking about that yet. Are you guys not worried about our final test? There is so much to study for Mrs. Kim's class, and I 4. missed class quite a few times... I want to get a good grade, but I don't know where to start.

Erica: I think you ought to talk to her. Maybe she can help you set up a study plan. And 5. why don't you join us over the weekend? We will have a group study session at Tiffiny's place.

Marco: Oh, thanks for the advice. I think you are right. I will talk to Mrs. Kim and definitely join you guys over the weekend. I hate studying alone!

Substitution Drill: Use the following responses in the above conversation.

		A. FORMAL	B. INFORMAL
1.	we booked the flights.	we made all the flight reservations.	we reserved the airline tickets.
2.	Do you have any suggestions?	What do you recommend?	What would you do?
3.	I hadn't thought about that.	I forgot to research that.	I didn't think about that.
4.	missed class quite a few times	didn't manage to make it to many classes	wasn't in enough classes
5.	why don't you join us over the weekend?	do you want to join us at the weekend?	you are welcome to join us over the weekend.

Grammar Gallery 2: *Giving & asking for advice:*

1. There are many ways to ask for advice, recommendation or help. Simply saying "Help me" is one way, but it may seem very direct, or impolite. In general, using one of the following forms will seem both polite and respectful.
(충고나 추천 또는 도움을 요청하는 방법이 많습니다. 단순히 "도와 줘"라고 말하는 것도 한 가지 방법이 될 수 있겠지만 너무 직접적이고 무례하게 보일 수 있습니다. 일반적으로 다음 도표에 나오는 표현 가운데 하나를 사용하는 것이 정중하게 예의에 맞습니다.)

Asking for advice	
• My parents are visiting Seoul for 4 days. • I need to lose 10 kg before the summer. • The final test is tomorrow and I don't have any notes in my book. • I think a fellow student is going to cheat on the test.	• What should I do? • What do you suggest? • Could you recommend something? • Do you have any suggestions? • What would you do? • Can you give me some advice? • Would you mind helping me?

2. As well, there are many ways to give advice, with different verbs for different degrees of intensity. In the following chart, notice how some verbs are followed by infinitives ***(to go, to leave...)***, gerunds ***(going, leaving...)*** or verb base forms ***(go, be...)***.
(또한 충고를 할 때에도 다른 동사를 사용하여 강도의 차이를 줄 수 있는 방법이 많습니다. 다음 도표에서 어떻게 일부 동사 뒤에 부정사가 따라오기도 하고 동명사가 따라오기도 하고 동사원형이 따라 오는가 주의해서 보세요.)
In general, giving suggestions (i.e. green box) rather than orders or strong recommendations (i.e. red box) is considered more polite and respectful.
(일반적으로 명령을 한다거나 강하게 권고 (빨간색 박스)를 하는 것보다 제안을 하는 것 (즉 녹색 박스)이 더 정중하고 예의를 갖춘 것으로 간주됩니다.)

Giving advice		
Strong advice, orders	• You must • You have to • You need to	call 911.
Recommendations	• You should • You ought to • You had better	ask the teacher.
Suggestions, More polite recommendations	• You could • Why don't you	search on the internet. search on the internet?
	• How about • Have you thought about	searching on the internet?

Exercise 8 *Match the sentences on the left asking for advice with those on the right giving recommendations.*

1. Our house is on fire, could you help me? ______
2. My tooth hurts, what should I do? ______
3. I have an English final next week! ______
4. This camera is too expensive. What would you do? ______
5. I need to study but I cannot focus at home. ______
6. My son is sick. Do you have any advice? ______
7. I want to improve my English listening skills. ______
8. My neighbors are so loud, I cannot sleep. ______

- A. You should stay home and study.
- B. How about watching English movies?
- C. I think you ought to stay home with him.
- D. You must call 911.
- E. Have you thought about talking to them?
- F. You had better go see a dentist.
- G. Why don't you go to the library?
- H. You could look on the internet.

Exercise 9 *Giving advice. Finish the sentences.*

1. A: I have a test tomorrow, but I didn't study!

   B: Why don't you ______________________________?

2. A: I want to get a driver's license. What should I do?

   B: Why don't you ______________________________?

3. A: My skin looks bad these days. What could I do to make it better?

   B: Why don't you ______________________________?

4. A: I think my girlfriend is mad at me. Should I just break up with her?

   B: How about ______________________________?

5. A: I was up all night working at my part-time job. I'm exhausted!

   B: How about ______________________________?

6. A: I'm so hungry, but I forgot my wallet. Could you buy me lunch?

B: ____ ?

7. A: We are going to Italy next summer! What should we do first?

B: ____ ?

8. A: I'm going to visit my grandmother in Miami. What should I pack?

B: ____ ?

9. A: Can I use the bathroom? It's an emergency!

B: ____ ?

10. A: I try hard but I still have difficulty speaking English. What should I do?

B: ____ ?

Exercise 10 *Read the following advice, and write an appropriate question / statement.* *(다음의 충고를 읽고 적합한 질문이나 문장을 작성해 보세요.)*

- You could look for a Chinese language academy.
- How about getting a massage?
- Maybe you should eat healthier food.
- You must take him to the hospital!
- You could move into a smaller apartment.
- You should take the phone to a KT A.S. center.
- Have you thought about getting a pet?
- You ought to take a taxi.

1. I need to learn Chinese. What should I do?
2. ____
3. ____
4. ____
5. ____
6. ____
7. ____

Exercise 11 *Dear Abby is a famous newspaper column in the U.S.A. where people write to and ask for advice. Read the following in a group and think of some advice.*

(Dear Abby는 독자들이 조언을 구하기 위해 편지를 써서 보내는 미국에서 유명한 신문 기사입니다. 조별로 다음 내용을 읽고 어떤 조언을 해 줄 수 있는지 생각해 보세요.)

1. Dear Abby,

My boyfriend thinks he is a good dresser, but his fashion is terrible! He spends a lot of money on clothes, but he has no style. I want to help him coordinate his clothes better, but I'm afraid of hurting his pride. Could you give me some advice?

– Dating GD

2. Dear Abby,

My friends are always asking to borrow money, and they never pay me back. I am bad at saying no to them, because they don't ask for a lot of money. But I think they should still pay me back. I am afraid of looking petty. What should I do?

– Money Tree

3. Dear Abby,

I work at Outback Steakhouse. I like my part-time job, because the manager is nice. I recommended my best friend when my manager told me he needed more workers. However, my best friend is not a good worker. He is never on time. He is always taking long bathroom breaks. He is also stealing food from the kitchen! I'm tired of lying for him, but he's my good friend. Plus, I'm the person who recommended him to my boss. I'm afraid of getting fired. What should I do?

– Nervous at Outback

4. Dear Abby,

I have a friend of a friend that I met through facebook. He does not know me. We never met before, because he lives in New York and I live in Seoul. We chat all the time online. I like him, and I think he likes me, too. Last week, he told me that he wants to visit me in Seoul! I'm excited about meeting him, but I'm also nervous. My photos on facebook are not very honest. I'm very good at photoshop. I'm afraid he might not recognize me. What should I do? Should I meet him?

– Photoshop

5. Dear Abby,

I'm thinking about moving closer to school. I found a clean apartment that I can afford. I also found a roommate who wants to move in as soon as possible. The problem is I didn't tell my mom. My mom is always nagging me. I'm tired of being careful around her. I'm afraid of asking for her permission, because she will probably say no. Should I just move out and apologize later?

– Confused

Phrasal Verbs using "BE":

Note, you need to change the "be" verb to "am", "is", "are", "was", and "were"

Phrasal Verb	Meaning	Example
Be off	**a.** When you leave some place, you can tell the people who are staying "I'm off" to let them know you are leaving. (어떤 장소를 떠날 때 남아있는 사람들에게 "저는 갑니다"라고 말을 하면 당신이 떠난다는 것을 알려주는 것입니다.)	**a.** I'm off to the lake for the weekend.
Be under the weather	**a.** When you are a little sick, maybe a cold or the flu, but not something too serious, you can say you are "under the weather" (심하지는 않고 감기 같은 것 때문에 좀 아플 때 "몸이 좀 좋지 않아"라고 말할 수 있습니다.)	**a.** I think I will pass on soccer. I am bit under the weather today.
Be taken aback	**a.** When you are surprised, mostly when the surprise is not very pleasant, you can say you were "taken aback" (유쾌하지 않게 놀랐을 때 "깜짝 놀랐어"라고 말할 수 있습니다.)	**a.** She was taken aback by the student's wonderful answers.
Be over the moon	**a.** When you are very, very happy, you can say you are "over the moon". (아주 행복할 때 "날아갈 것 같아"라고 말할 수 있습니다.)	**a.** She is over the moon with her new promotion.

Be into	a. When you enjoy, and are interested in a subject, artist, style… you can say you are "into" it. (즐기고 있거나 어떤 주제나 예술 또는 스타일에 관심이 있을 때 "난 거기에 빠졌어"라고 말할 수 있습니다.)	a. He is really into K-Pop these days. He is always listening to that kind of music.
Be in	a. When you agree to participate in a project or idea, you can say you are "in" (어떤 사업이나 생각에 참여하기로 동의할 때 "나도 동감이야."라고 말할 수 있습니다.)	a. A: Who will help me with the Smith project next week? B: I'm in. I would love to help.
Be out	a. The opposite of "be in" ("be in"의 반대말입니다.) b. Similar meaning to "be off" with a sense of immediacy, as if you are already gone. ("be off"와 비슷한 의미를 지니지만 이미 가고 없는 것처럼 긴급함을 강조합니다.)	a. A: Can you still come this weekend? B: Sorry, I'm out. I have to do something else. b. I'm out of the office this afternoon. Please change my schedule.

Exercise 12 *Complete these example sentences with the correct phrasal verbs. You have to use the correct form of the verb "be" ➡ (am / is / are / was / were)*

1. *Michelle:* Okay, we are hiking Mt. Seorak tomorrow, leaving Seoul at midnight to avoid traffic. Who's in?
   Wei: That sounds great! I __________ __________ !
   Marco: Oh, no. I have too much to do over the weekend.
2. *Erika:* So, what kind of sports do you like? Well, I __________ really winter sports, like skiing and snowboarding.
3. *P.K.:* I __________ totally when he told me his mother had just passed away!
   Wei: I can imagine, what a shock!
4. *Wei:* I think I need to stay home today, I __________ feeling a little .
   Tiffiny: Oh, sorry to hear that. I hope you feel better tomorrow.
5. *Erika:* Congratulations on winning the 1st place! I'm so happy for you. You must be so happy!
   Marco: I __________ just ____________________ .
6. *Michelle:* Wei, are you leaving already?
   Wei: Yes, I __________ . I need to catch the last bus home!

TOEIC VOCABULARY

Read the following common TOEIC words. Memorize so that you can do well on the TOEIC. Write the Korean and English in the space below two times to help you learn.

According to: ~에 따르면, ~에 따라.
Workers are paid according to the amount of work they do from nine to six.
근로자들은 9시부터 6시까지 하는 업무량에 따라 보수를 받는다.

_________ / _________ _________ / _________

Accordingly: 따라서.
People still consider me a child and treat me accordingly.
사람들은 아직도 나를 어린애로 간주하고 그렇게 대우한다.
Some of the labor laws are contradictory. Accordingly, measures should be taken to clarify them.
노동법의 일부는 모순이 있다. 따라서 모순을 수정하기 위한 조치가 취해져야 한다.

_________ / _________ _________ / _________

Account for: 차지하다, 설명하다.
As of 2016, foreigners account for 10% of the Korean population.
2016년 현재 한국의 인구 중 외국인이 10%를 차지한다.

_________ / _________ _________ / _________

Accumulate: 축적하다.
It is against public expectation that a privileged few continue to accumulate most of the wealth.
소수 특권층이 계속 대부분의 부를 쌓아간다는 것은 대중의 기대와 어긋난다.

_________ / _________ _________ / _________

Acknowledge: 인정하다.
Many local companies acknowledge the need for change.
많은 현지 기업들이 변화의 필요성을 인정한다.

_________ / _________ _________ / _________

Acquaint: 친숙하게 하다.
Students need to acquaint themselves with the new regulations.
학생들은 새로운 규정에 친숙할 필요가 있다.

_________ / _________ _________ / _________

Acquire: 획득하다.
Consumers want to acquire valuable goods as cheaply as possible.
소비자들은 가능한 저렴하게 가치 있는 상품을 구입하고 싶어한다.

_________ / _________ _________ / _________

Additional: 추가적인.
An additional charge is made on luggage exceeding the weight allowance.
중량 허용치를 초과하는 수하물에는 추가 요금이 부과됩니다.

_________ / _________ _________ / _________

Adequate: 적절한.
You have yet to provide an adequate explanation for your actions.
당신의 행위에 대해 적절한 설명을 해야 합니다.

_________ / _________ _________ / _________

Affect: 영향을 끼치다.
The economy will be adversely affected by the downturn in consumer spending.
소비자 지출 감소 때문에 경제가 악영향을 받을 것이다.

_________ / _________ _________ / _________

Agreement: 동의, 계약.
Did your boss have an agreement with the union as to when to raise salary?
사장님은 임금 인상 시기에 관해 노조와 동의를 했나요?

_________ / _________ _________ / _________

Alert: 경계하는.
Taking notes is one of the best ways to stay alert in lectures.
필기하는 것이 강의 중에 집중할 수 는 최상의 방법이다.

_________ / _________ _________ / _________

Alleviate: 완화시키다.
Politicians must come up with some measures to alleviate poverty.
정치인들은 빈곤을 완화시킬 수 있는 조치를 내놓아야 한다.

_________ / _________ _________ / _________

Allocate: 할당하다.
Students should be able to allocate the same amount of time to each question.
학생들은 모든 문제에 동일한 시간을 할애할 수 있어야 한다.

_________ /_________ _________ /_________

Anticipate: 기대하다.
A good speaker should anticipate an audience's needs and concerns.
좋은 연설자는 청중의 욕구와 관심사를 기대해야 한다.

_________ /_________ _________ /_________

Applaud: 칭찬하다.
Most of us applauded the decision to install more security cameras all over the premises.
우리 대부분은 구내 전 지역에 더 많은 보안용 카메라를 설치하기로 한 결정을 칭찬했다.

_________ /_________ _________ /_________

Appoint: 지명하다.
A committee was appointed to review the plans.
계획을 검토하기 위한 위원회가 지명되었다.

_________ /_________ _________ /_________

Appropriate: 적합한.
It would not be appropriate for you and me to discuss that now.
그 문제를 지금 너와 내가 토론하는 것은 적절하지 않을 것이다.

_________ /_________ _________ /_________

Approximately: 대략.
The plane will be taking off in approximately 10 minutes.
비행기는 대략 10분 뒤에 이륙할 것이다.

_________ /_________ _________ /_________

Asset: 자산.
A sense of duty is a great asset in any business.
의무감은 어떤 사업을 할 때라도 커다란 자산이다.

_________ /_________ _________ /_________

Assume: 가정하다.
I didn't see your car, so I assumed you'd already left for Seoul.
네 차가 보이지 않아서 네가 이미 서울로 떠났다고 생각했어.

_________ /_________ _________ /_________

Astonish: 놀라게 하다.
It astonished all of us that she had changed so much.
그녀가 너무 많이 변해서 우리 모두 놀랐다.

_________ /_________ _________ /_________

Attribute: ~의 탓(책임, 덕택)으로 돌리다.
The fall in the number of deaths from avian influenza is largely attributed to the development of new medicine.
조류 독감으로 인한 사망자 수가 감소한 것은 대체로 신약 개발 덕택이다.

_________ /_________ _________ /_________

Authorize: 권한을 위임하다.
The mayor of Seoul authorized several companies to rebuild the Magok Area.
서울 시장은 몇 개 기업에게 마곡 지구 재개발을 위한 권한을 부여했다.

_________ /_________ _________ /_________

Award: 상.
Hotel Shilla's award-winning restaurant specializes in traditional Korean food.
신라호텔의 수상 경력이 있는 식당은 전통한식을 전문으로 한다.

_________ /_________ _________ /_________

Beneficial: 이로운.
Riding a bicycle is highly beneficial to our health and the environment.
자전거를 타면 우리의 건강과 환경에 매우 이롭다.

_________ /_________ _________ /_________

Branch: 나뭇가지, 지사.
They're planning to open a new branch in San Diego next year.
그들은 내년에 San Diego에 새로운 지사를 설치할 계획이다.

_________ /_________ _________ /_________

Candidate: 후보자
Candidates are not allowed to use any mechanic device in this exam.
후보자들은 이번 시험에서 어떤 기계 장치도 사용할 수 없다.

_________ /_________ _________ /_________

Capable: ~할 능력이 있는.
The company isn't capable of handling such a large order.
회사는 이렇게 대규모의 주문을 처리할 능력이 없다.

_________ /_________ _________ /_________

Career: 경력, 취업.
Beating the incumbent congressman is the high point of my career.
현직 국회의원을 물리친 것이 내 경력의 최고 순간이다.

_________ /_________ _________ /_________

UNIT 6-10 REVIEW

Warm-up Questions:

Exercise 1 *Answer the questions, using complete sentences.*

16. What is your daily routine?

17. What things do you need to do every day?

18. What things do you want to do every day?

19. What are your skills? What are you good at? What can you do well?

20. What can your father do well? Mother?

21. What do you want to be able to do in the future?

22. What are you bad at? What can't you do well?

23. What's your favorite kind of weather? Why?

24. What is your favorite season? What do you do in that season?

25. What are your goals? What do you need to do to attain your goal?

26. What will you do if you attain your dream?

27. What will you do if you can't attain your dream?

28. Why do you study English?

29. How can speaking English be helpful in your future?

30. How can you continue to study English on your own?

Conversation Corner: *In What Order?*

Exercise 2 *ORDER the sentences with ORDINAL NUMBERS (1st, 2nd, 3rd, 4th, 5th…). The first two are done for you. Susan's sentences are in orange, and Kevin's sentences are in blue.*

_____ Hmm… I had pasta last night. Does either of them have steak?

_____ Well, do you like pasta? Alberto's spaghetti is better than The Big Oven's spaghetti.

1st Hey Kevin, are you busy?

_____ Hi Susan, not at all. What's up?

Yes, they both have steak. The Big Oven definitely has the best steak.

_____ I think we will go to the Big Oven then. Thanks for your advice!

_____ No problem! Have a great night out with your friend!

_____ My friend from Borneo is visiting me. I want to take her to a really good restaurant. I was considering Alberto's Pasta Place, but I also heard that The Big Oven has excellent food. Which is best?

Exercise 3 *Respond to the following questions FOR YOU. You can look back in the book to each chapter if necessary.*

(다음의 질문에 대해 자신의 견해로 대답하세요. 필요하다면 본문 각 장을 참고하세요.)

1. In your opinion, what is the best movie?	
2. Are movies better than books?	
3. Who is the funniest person in your family?	
4. Are you going to go to your hometown this Christmas?	
5. What sport do you love?	
6. What do you plan to do this weekend?	
7. What do you want to do this weekend?	

Grammar Gallery: *Comparative and Superlative Review*

Exercise 4 *Comparatives and superlatives: Complete the following exercises by circling the correct "comparative" or "superlative".*

(비교급과 최상급: 정확한 비교급과 최상급에 원을 그려서 연습문제를 완성하세요.)

1. Cheetahs are faster / slower than turtles.
2. Tea is colder / hotter than milk.
3. Your mother is older / younger than you.
4. Mt. Everest is the taller / the tallest mountain peak.
5. Balloons are lighter / heavier than bowling balls.
6. Diamonds are more expensive / expensiver than rubies.
7. Jalapenos are hotter / hottest than pickles.
8. Anacondas are longer / taller than alligators.
9. Vegetables are healthier / healthiest than chocolate bars.
10. Snowy days are badder / worse than rainy days.

Exercise 5 *Complete the comparative sentences, using the picture below.*

1. The ______________ is taller than the ______________ .

2. The ______________ is shorter than the ______________ .

3. The ______________ is bigger than the ______________ .

4. The ______________ is scarier than the ______________ .

5. The ______________ is cuter than the ______________ .

6. The ______________ is heavier than the ______________ .

7. The ______________ is lighter than the ______________ .

8. The ______________ is smaller than the ______________ .

Exercise 6 Let's Play Trivia!

Form groups of 4, and answer the questions below. Then, compare your answers with another group, and search online (in English!) for the answers. Good luck!
(4명이 한 조를 만들어서 아래 질문에 답해 보세요. 그리고 나서 다른 조와 대답을 비교해 보고 영문 인터넷으로 답을 찾아보세요.)

What is the tallest building in the world?	What city has the most people?
What is the smallest planet?	What is the biggest planet?
What is the fastest land animal?	What country is the largest?
What is the deepest ocean?	What is the longest wall?
What animal has the biggest egg?	What is the highest mountain peak?
What is the longest day of the year?	What is the tallest animal?
Who is the tallest student in the class?	Who is the youngest student in the class?
Who has the biggest backpack / bag in the class?	Bonus: Who is the best professor?

Exercise 7 *"A Bad Day": Complete the story: In the following paragraph, complete the sentences, using "past continuous affirmative" phrases. The first one is done for you.*

I was having a bad day today. When I *(shave)* was shaving, I cut my face! Now I have pieces of tissue all over my face. Then, when I ______ ______ *(drink)* coffee, I spilled some on my new tie! I changed my tie, and went outside to catch the bus. But while I ______ ______ *(wait)*, it started to rain! I didn't have an umbrella, so I got very wet. Finally, I got on the bus. I ______ ______ *(play)* a game on my phone, and I ______ ______ *(win)*! That made me happy. But guess what? I was so excited, I missed my bus stop! I wished I ______ still ______ *(sleep)* in bed.

Exercise 8 *Past Continuous: Negative and Questions: Answer the questions in the negative, and provide an alternate answer.*

Ex. Were you watching T.V. last night?

No, I wasn't. I was playing chess with my brother.

1. Were you playing phone games in class?

____

2. Was she crying because she lost an earring?

____

3. I saw you at a restaurant last night. Were you celebrating your wedding anniversary?

____

4. Was I being too loud at the movie theater?

____

5. You didn't finish your coffee. Was it too bitter for you?

____

6. Was the weather good for your picnic yesterday?

____

7. I bought concert tickets at the stadium. Were they cheaper online?

____

8. You look wet. Was it raining when you were walking to work?

____

Exercise 9 *"Past Continuous" vs. "Past Simple": Ask a classmate the following questions, and write down their answers, using either past continuous, or past simple, in full sentences.*

1. What did you eat for lunch yesterday?

2. What were you doing during the break?

3. Did you study for the quiz today?

4. What time did you go to sleep last night?

5. How did you come to class today?

6. Did you brush your teeth this morning?

7. Were you a diligent student in high school?

8. Who was your best friend in elementary school?

9. What were you doing last night?

10. What was the most popular song last summer?

Exercise 10 Future Tense: What will you do on Saturday?

Write down 5-10 ideas that you will or won't do this Saturday. For example, 'Do laundry' or 'Not do laundry'. Don't worry about the grammar at this point, only ideas.
(이번 주 토요일에 하고 싶은/하고 싶지 않은 일에 대한 5개 내지 10개의 생각을 써 보세요. 예를 들면 "빨래하기", 또는 "빨래하지 않기." 문법에 구애 받지 마세요. 생각만 나열하는 것입니다.)

Now write these ideas in full sentences to form a paragraph.
(이제 그 생각들을 완벽한 문장으로 작성하여 하나의 문단을 만들어 보세요.)

Exercise 11 *Future Tense, using "be going to (verb)": Unscramble and write the phrases to form correct sentences. HINT: Look for the capitalized words and punctuation!*

1. going to / I am / my aunt's house. / go to

2. make a /going to / You are / mess!

3. You are / have a / the Philippines! / going to / time / great / in

4. your laundry? / When / going / to do / are you

______

5. It is / today. / rain / definitely going to

______

6. I am / exam. / going to / study all night / English / for my

______

7. if / They are / crash / going to / they / that fast. / drive

______

8. grandmother / I'm / call / going to / my / lunch. / after

______

9. summer. / We / going to / paint / are / house by the lake / our / this

______

10. grow / an astronaut. / up, / When / I'm / going to / I / be

______

Exercise 12 *Tag Questions, Present Simple and Past Simple: In the following questions, add a tag question to complete the sentence.*

1. You are Olivier's brother, ______ ?
2. The water looks pretty deep. You know how to swim, ______ ?
3. We're meeting at McDonald's, ______ ?
4. You weren't late for school, ______ ?
5. I'm making a cake. One cup of sugar is enough, ______ ?
6. There are so many people at this party. Erica is here too, ______ ?
7. You live near a hospital, ______ ?
8. Michelle is very funny, ______ ?
9. I ordered pizza. You like pepperoni, ______ ?
10. That movie was so boring, ______ ?

Exercise 13

Common Gerunds: Use a gerund from the box to complete the sentences below.

skydiving	singing	hiking	shopping	swimming
drawing	walking	kickboxing	dancing	smoking

1. She likes ______________ . She can dive very well!
2. ______________ is my favorite sport.
3. Do you dislike ______________? Then you won't like this movie. It's a musical.
4. I like singing, but I'm not good at ______________ .
5. You have so many pencils. You enjoy ______________ , don't you?
6. Your teeth are a little yellow. You should stop ______________ .
7. This forest is beautiful. I love ______________ here.
8. I don't take the bus to school. I prefer ______________ .
9. I got $50 for my birthday! Let's go ______________ !
10. I'm scared of heights. I don't want to go ______________ !

Exercise 14

Common Infinitives (need, want, promise, hope, plan): In the following sentences, circle the verbs that are commonly followed by infinitives. (일반적인 부정사 (need, want, promise, hope, plan): 다음 문장에서 일반적으로 부정사가 따라오는 동사에 원을 그리세요.)

1. I (promised) to take my girlfriend out for dinner.
2. I need to do my homework before I can watch T.V.
3. I want to get a good grade in my English class. I need to study more.
4. I like to golf, but I don't like watching golf.
5. Your secret is safe with me. I promise not to tell another person!
6. I had a great time tonight. I hope to see you again!
7. I'm making soup. You can cut some vegetables, if you want to help.
8. I need to go to the store. Is there anything you need?
9. I planned to finish my report by today, but it's already 11 p.m.!
10. Do you want to build a snowman?

New Grammar: Subordinating Conjunctions

'Subordinating conjunctions' tie together a dependent clause and an independent clause, although not necessarily in any particular order. There are many subordinating conjunctions in the English language; however, some common ones are:

("종속접속사"는 꼭 특별한 순서를 따르지는 않으면서 종속절과 주절을 연결해 줍니다. 영어에는 종속접속사가 많이 있습니다; 하지만 일반적으로 사용되는 것들은 다음과 같은 것들입니다.)

After (~하고 나서) / although (~에도 불구하고) / because (왜냐하면)
even though (비록 ~하더라도) / since (~이기 때문에, ~이후에) / rather than (~보다는 오히려)

For example, "I didn't go to the beach today because it was raining."
(예를 들면 "비가 왔기 때문에 나는 해변에 가지 않았다.")

Exercise 15 *Subordinating Conjunctions In the following sentences, use one of the subordinating conjunctions listed above. Note: sometimes there is more than one possible answer!*
(다음 문장에서 위에 나와 있는 종속접속사 중 하나를 사용하세요. 주의사항: 때로는 하나 이상의 답이 있을 수도 있습니다.)

1. ______________ it wasn't her fault, she still felt bad.
2. I didn't want to eat the soup ______________ it had oysters in it.
3. ______________ she went to work, I turned on my music, and played it loud!
4. ______________ the road construction, I had to take a different route home.
5. I would like to watch a movie ______________ go to a coffee shop.
6. I will never be a doctor ______________ I cannot look at blood without fainting!
7. I'm having a great day ______________ you are here.
8. I have a lot of homework to do ______________ I can meet you for a bit.*

CULTURAL NOTE: 'a bit' can be used when talking about a small amount, such as "I would like a little bit of cake", but it can also be used to substitute for a short period of time. For example, "I will be a bit late for work."
('a bit' 은 "케이크를 좀 먹고 싶네"와 같이 소량에 대해 말할 때 사용할 수 있지만 잠깐 동안의 시간을 가리킬 때에도 사용될 수 있습니다. 예를 들어 "나는 출근이 좀 늦을 것 같습니다.")